DISCARD

W9-CJO-019

snacking cakes

Simple Treats for
Anytime Cravings

snacking
cakes

Yossy Arefi

Photo Styling by Ali Slagle

Clarkson Potter/Publishers
New York

Copyright © 2020 by Yasameen Arefi-Afshar

All rights reserved.
Published in the United States by Clarkson Potter/
Publishers, an imprint of Random House, a division of
Penguin Random House LLC, New York.
clarksonpotter.com

CLARKSON POTTER is a trademark and POTTER with
colophon is a registered trademark of Penguin Random
House LLC.

Library of Congress Cataloging-in-Publication Data is
available upon request

ISBN 978-0-593-13966-0
Ebook ISBN 978-0-593-13967-7

Printed in Germany

Book design by Mia Johnson
Photographs by Yossy Arefi

10 9 8 7 6 5 4 3 2 1

First Edition

To anyone who needs a snack

contents

introduction

So, what exactly makes a cake a snacking cake? I certainly didn't invent the concept, and it depends a little bit on who you ask, but to me a snacking cake is a single layer cake, probably square, covered with a simple icing—or nothing at all—and it must be truly easy to make. It's a cake that makes an ideal breakfast to-go, wrapped in a paper napkin, and a perfect little sweet to have alongside coffee in the afternoon.

These cakes are the kind of baking I love—they are low stress and don't require much besides a reasonably stocked pantry, a bowl, and a whisk. These aren't the kind of all-day project bakes you'll see on *The Great British Baking Show*; rather, they are humble everyday treats that can lift your spirit and satisfy your hunger for something sweet, at any time of day. These are the sort of cakes you can throw together after work on a weeknight with minimal effort, minimal time, and minimal mess.

Snacking cakes can be cut into tidy little squares and tucked into lunch boxes or wrapped up in a sheet of beeswax food wrap to gift to a friend who has just moved into a new apartment, so they have something for dessert that night, and breakfast the next morning. They are the sort of cakes that help celebrate the large and small moments of life. Even if that moment is just making it through work on a Monday.

These are also the perfect kinds of recipes for little hands to help with. Since everything basically gets thrown into the same bowl, if your tiny assistant gets overzealous and adds the ingredients a little out of order, nothing too terrible will happen, theoretically. . . .

I've tried to hit every possible cake craving in these 50 recipes, from bright, citrusy olive oil cakes to fudgy chocolate ones, to fruit- and veggie-(yes, veggie!)packed cakes with seedy toppings and naturally technicolor glazes or fluffy frostings. There are lots of variations, too, and you have my full encouragement to make these cakes your own. You can combine the cakes and toppings in any way you see fit, and if glazes or frostings seem too fussy, these cakes are all perfectly delicious with a simple dusting of confectioners' sugar—or nothing at all.

It's a simple luxury to bake a snacking cake for yourself or your friends and family. I hope this book inspires you to do it often, and with abandon.

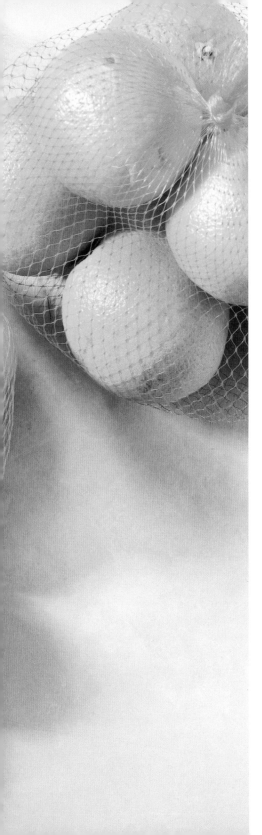

the method

In the spirit of making these cakes super-easy, anytime treats, almost all of them can be made in just one bowl. Yes, there are instances when you'll need a second bowl to make a crispy crumb topping or a little saucepan to brown some butter (only a few, I promise!), but I wouldn't ask you to do it if it wasn't worth it.

Some of the these recipes come together so quickly that your oven might not even have time to heat up before the batter is ready to go. Make sure to give your oven a few minutes' head start so it has time to reach 350°F.

There is a time and place for creaming butter and sugar until it's light and fluffy, adding eggs one at a time—but, folks, this isn't it. These cakes do not require any creaming or electric equipment, but you'll have to pay special attention to make sure your batters are evenly mixed.

Most of the cakes start by quickly and vigorously whisking the eggs and sugar together, which combines these two ingredients and starts to dissolve the sugar. You're looking for the mix to thicken slightly and turn a nice pale yellow.

After the sugar and eggs are combined, add the oil or butter and any liquids, purees, and/or flavorings, then whisk everything together until smooth and emulsified.

If your cake calls for cocoa powder, it goes in before the other dry ingredients, so you can give that cocoa a strong stir to break up any lumps without risk of overmixing the batter. If your cocoa is super lumpy, it is a good idea to sift it into the mix; either way, just make sure the cocoa is smooth before you add the flour.

Finally, add the flour and leavening agent, and mix the batter until it is well-combined and smooth. Use the edge of the whisk to scrape the bottom and sides of the bowl to ensure even mixing. If the batter is thick, you can switch to a rubber spatula for those last few strokes. Then, any mix-ins, like chocolate chips, dried fruits, or nuts, are folded in just before you pour the batter into the pan.

some notes on baking pans

I recommend light-colored metal baking pans rather than glass or ceramic for these cakes. USA Pans and Nordic Ware both make high-quality sturdy baking pans that will last a long time. Nordic Ware also makes an incredible variety of beautiful Bundt pans.

Every baker has a favorite way to prepare baking pans, and I find that a thin coat of butter or nonstick cooking spray and a strip or round of parchment paper does the most consistent job for these cakes. Some recipes call for lining the cake pans with nuts or seeds, too, which lends a little extra texture and flavor.

how to dress up
a cake

You'll find that these cakes are super flavorful on their own, but there are times when a glaze or frosting makes them even better. Most of the glazes in this book are made by simply whisking all of the glaze ingredients until smooth. Just like the cakes themselves, they are quick and easy to make, but if you aren't feeling the glaze or you're short on time, these cakes are just fine with a simple dusting of confectioners' sugar or even nothing at all. Personally, I can never resist a crackly layer of glaze, especially if it's citrusy, but the toppings are always optional.

That said, feel free to mix and match the cakes and toppings to suit your tastes! The combinations given here are just a guide to get you started. Combine your favorite flavors—I wouldn't dare try to stop you.

I've also included lots of fun ideas to take these simple cakes from the snack bar to the dessert table. You'll find recipes for flavored whipped creams (pages 178 to 182) and suggested toppings (fresh fruit, shaved chocolate, crushed pretzels, cornflakes—oh my!) to dress them up for a party. Ice cream is never a bad idea.

round pans, bundts, loaves, and more

You can bake any cake in this book in an 8-inch square baking pan, the classic snacking cake pan. In the recipe notes, however, you'll see some suggestions for baking these cakes in different pans if the mood strikes.

Here are some general guidelines for using other pan types, if you'd like to get even more creative.

Round: You can also bake any of these recipes in a 9-inch round cake pan. Just make sure it is at least 2 inches tall. Butter or coat the pan with nonstick spray and line the bottom of the pan with a round of parchment paper. Don't worry about making a parchment sling; the parchment round should be sufficient to ensure the cake doesn't stick. The baking time for a 9-inch pan is similar to that for the 8-inch square. After the cake has cooled for about 15 minutes, run a thin knife around the edge and carefully turn the cake out onto a cooling rack, then invert it again so it is puffy side up, if desired.

Loaf: You can also bake most of these recipes in a 9 x 5 x 3-inch loaf pan. Butter or coat the pan with nonstick spray and line the pan with a strip of parchment paper that hangs over the two long sides. Add 10 to 20 minutes to the baking time to compensate for the additional thickness. Take extra care to make sure your loaf is baked all the way through, as judging doneness on a loaf cake can be a little tricky. See the tips on pages 16 to 17 for help on your way to loaf success.

Skillet: Some cakes are just lovely baked in a skillet. Generously butter or coat a 9-inch

oven-safe skillet with nonstick spray and line the bottom of the skillet with a round of parchment paper. Don't worry about making a parchment sling; the round should be enough to ensure the cake doesn't stick. The baking time for a skillet is similar to that for the 8-inch square. After the cake has cooled for about 15 minutes, run a thin knife around the edge of the pan. You can invert it onto a rack to cool or let it cool in the skillet and serve it from there.

Sheet: If you are having a party and want more cake, or if you just need more cake in your life than an 8-inch square provides, you can double most of these recipes and bake them in a 9 x 13-inch pan. Take care to not fill the pan too much; you should leave at least 1 inch of space at the top of the pan for the batter to rise. Butter or coat the pan with nonstick spray and line it with a strip of parchment paper that hangs over the two long sides. Add 5 to 15 minutes to the bake time (see the tips on page 16 to tell if your cake is baked through). Let the cake cool for 15 minutes, then use the parchment sling to carefully lift the cake out of the pan onto a rack to cool completely. You can also let the cake cool in the pan and serve it from there. Note: It's tricky to multiply the ingredients for the upside-down cakes, so I don't suggest doubling those recipes to bake in a sheet pan.

Bundt: You can double most of these recipes and bake them in a 15-cup Bundt pan, but make sure you don't overfill the pan. Each recipe yields a slightly different volume of batter, so make sure that there is at least 2 inches of empty space at the top of the pan. If you find you have a little more batter than your pan can handle, pour it into a prepared ramekin or small pan, rather than trying to fit it all in the Bundt pan. Take it from me: Scraping burnt cake batter off the bottom of your oven is not something you ever want to have to do.

To prep a Bundt pan, thoroughly coat each crack and crevice with a thin, even layer of very soft butter (I use a pastry brush for this), and then dust evenly with flour and knock out the excess. Bake the cake for an additional 15 to 30 minutes and use a long skewer inserted into the thickest part to test whether the cake is baked through. Let the cake cool in the pan for 15 minutes on a rack, then carefully invert it onto the rack to cool completely. Don't let the cake cool completely in the pan—that is a one-way ticket to a stuck cake and lots of frustration. All that said, if you have a different method that works for you, keep using it. I would never want to mess with someone's tried-and-true Bundt pan preparation system. Note: The cakes with nut, seed, or fruit toppings aren't great candidates for a Bundt cake.

Cupcakes: I admit that I do not have much love for cupcakes after working in a bakery for many years and baking thousands of them. I find them quite fussy to portion and decorate (let's not even talk about trying to transport them!). But if you like a little cake in a paper cup, these recipes each make 12 to 18 regular-size cupcakes. I recommend using paper liners and not filling the cups more than halfway. The cupcakes will take 12 to 18 minutes to bake, but take care not to overbake them or they will be dry. Also, don't be surprised if they don't have perfect little domed tops when baked through. Some recipes will, and some won't.

doubling a recipe

If you are multiplying a recipe, make sure you use a large bowl to mix the batter—something around 6 quarts is ideal. A large bowl will allow lots of room to move when you are mixing and folding, and it will reduce the chance of overmixing your batter and making the cake dense. If you find your whisk is getting stuck in the batter, switch to a rubber spatula and start folding.

If you're making a glaze or frosting for a cake recipe you have doubled, you'll also want to double the glaze ingredients. For loaf cakes, cut the glaze or frosting recipes in half.

how can you tell when a cake is done?

Being able to read a few visual cues is really important for cake baking success. A fully baked cake will be puffy and will spring back when lightly pressed. Lighter colored batters (i.e., not chocolate) will be golden, especially around the edges.

A fully baked cake will also pull away from the edges of the pan ever so slightly, and a toothpick or skewer inserted into the thickest part will come out clean or with a few moist crumbs attached. If your cake is still a little soggy after the baking time called for in the recipe, bake it for a few more minutes, then check again. Ovens vary! Pans vary! Life happens! Your cake should also smell sweet, toasty, and delicious.

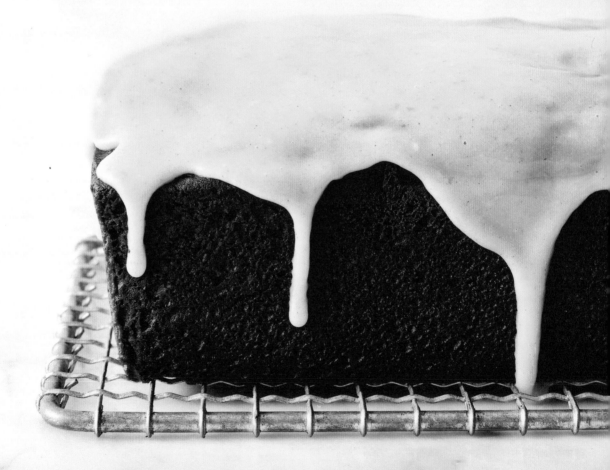

Loaf and Bundt cakes can be a little tricky to test for doneness because the cakes are so thick. Make sure to check that the top and very center of the cake are cooked through and are dry in appearance. If the top still looks a little wet after the bake time called for in a recipe, give the cake another minute or two to make sure it is baked through. Sometimes the top will look set and puffed when the center is still underdone, so be sure to test for doneness with a long skewer that goes all the way to the bottom of the pan.

cake storage

When I have a snacking cake on my countertop, I sneak a little slice every time I walk by, so it never lasts more than a day or two. But here are some tips for longer-term storage, should you need them.

Most of these cakes keep best covered at room temperature for two to three days, but honestly, a few more days won't hurt, if your cake makes it that long. After the cake is cool, wrap it well with your food wrap of choice (I usually use aluminum foil or plastic wrap), or you can put it back in the pan it was baked in and cover the pan tightly for storage. If you wrap the cakes before they are completely cool, they will steam inside the wrapping and get a little soggy. Cakes with glaze or frosting can be covered loosely so the toppings don't stick to the wrapping.

Some of the glazes can get a little soft and wrinkly by the second day, but they are still perfectly delicious. Fruit cakes will also soften faster than their fruit-free counterparts. Some cakes are very tasty straight from the fridge, so in those cases I've noted that at the bottom of the recipe. Generally, cake also freezes exceptionally well, and you can store these cakes well-wrapped in a layer of plastic wrap and a layer of foil for up to a month.

all the equipment you really need

Baking Pans: All the recipes in this book were written with an 8-inch square pan in mind. I have a strong preference for baking cakes in light-colored metal pans, and my very favorites are the aluminized steel pans from USA Pans. Nordic Ware also makes nice uncoated aluminum pans. These pans are sturdy and high quality, and they should last you a lifetime. I steer away from glass or ceramic pans for cake baking, because they take longer to heat up, which means that the cakes don't bake as beautifully as they do in metal pans.

Cooling Rack: A wire rack is the ideal spot to let your cakes cool. Putting the cakes on a rack not only protects your countertops from hot pans but, more important, also allows air to circulate around the cakes, cooling them faster and, in turn, cutting down on the time you have to wait before digging in. Cooling on a rack instead of in the pan also helps your cakes keep their crunchy edges, and who doesn't love the crispy crunch of a corner slice of cake?

Fine-Mesh Sieve: You're probably going to want a fine-mesh sieve for all that confectioners' sugar dusting you are about to do. I am partial to the inexpensive stainless steel ones you can find at a restaurant-supply store. They are a great all-purpose tool, too—you'll find yourself reaching for your sieve to rinse grains and veggies, to drain pasta, and even to use as a steamer basket in a pinch.

Hand Mixer: An electric hand mixer will come in handy if you want to make the buttercream frostings in this book, but you won't specifically need it for any of the cakes or glazes. I've been using an inexpensive one I bought about ten years ago at my local hardware store. It doesn't have to be fancy to do the job.

Measuring Tools: A combination of measuring spoons and a scale is my preferred measuring method. It is more accurate than measuring cups, involves fewer dishes to wash, and helps you avoid having to scrape—a very annoying kitchen task if you ask me!—honey or thick sour cream out of a measuring cup or spoon. But if you are as passionate about your measuring cups as I am about my scale, I won't stop you. Measurements for both volume and weight are provided. I have an OXO digital scale with a pull-out display that I use almost every day. It's a bit of an investment, but if you are serious about baking and cooking, it is a worthwhile splurge.

Microplane: A Microplane is one of my very favorite kitchen tools, mostly because I am a citrus addict and can't resist adding a bit of lemon zest to pretty much everything I bake. I use it to zest citrus fruits, grate fresh ginger, and finely shave chocolate.

Mini Offset Spatula: This kitchen wonder does so much, where should I even start? I use it to smooth the top of cake batter before baking, loosen the sides of a baked cake while it is still in the pan, spread frosting or glaze, scoot cookies around a baking sheet, and lots more. You won't regret spending $5 or less on one, and you'll use it all the time. I like the 4½-inch ones made by Ateco.

Mixing Bowls: I prefer stainless steel bowls because they are light and sturdy, but glass and ceramic bowls are great, too. A 4- or 5-quart bowl is perfect for a single batch of cake batter. Something a little smaller is just fine for a batch of glaze, but honestly, I usually clean out my batter bowl and use it again for the glaze. No need to get two things out of the cabinet.

Oven Thermometer: If you are a frequent baker, an oven thermometer is one of the very best gifts you can give yourself. The temperature in some ovens, especially older models, can be off by enough degrees to make the baking experience very frustrating. It's worthwhile to pick one up for a few dollars next time you go to the kitchen shop. I keep one in my oven at all times.

Parchment Paper: The truth is, most of these cakes will slide right out of a well-greased pan, but I also like to line the pan with a piece of parchment paper.

Parchment paper is a nice little safety net, especially for cakes with chocolate or fruit folded into the batter. I keep a big box of pre-cut parchment sheets rather than a roll on hand, and I use them constantly—but use what you prefer. You can cut the individual sheets in half to make a little parchment sling for an 8-inch square pan or a 9 x 5 x 3-inch loaf pan. Use the full sheet to line a 9 x 13-inch pan.

Rubber/Silicone Spatula: A sturdy but flexible rubber spatula will help ensure your batters are evenly mixed and y our bowls are scraped clean. I am partial to the spatulas made by GIR and Le Creuset.

Whisk: A 10-inch balloon whisk is going to be your best friend. Make sure it has sturdy wires and a comfortable handle. OXO makes a great one. Did you catch how many times I said "sturdy" in this equipment list? I just want you to have the best possible tools for your baking adventures!

let's talk ingredients

I've learned in my many years of publishing recipes online with comment sections that people love to make substitutions, and I get it. I, too, sometimes can't bring myself to follow a recipe exactly as written, but there are certain times when a substitution makes sense and other times when it can get you into trouble.

Don't like walnuts? Use pecans instead. Not a fan of cardamom? Substitute a spice you like more, or leave it out altogether. Fruits that are in the same general family can usually be swapped—apples for pears, blueberries for blackberries, peaches for plums—with good results.

But if we are talking about structural changes to a recipe, such as substituting a different type of dairy or flour, changing the amount of sugar, increasing the leavening, or leaving out the eggs, use caution! I can't say for sure whether those swaps will work, but if you want to try something, I wish you luck on your journey.

I did my very best to keep the super-specific ingredients for these cakes to a minimum, as I wanted them to be weeknight friendly and not to call for a bunch of ingredients you'll use only once. I understand that not everyone keeps a super-stocked baking pantry, and the truth is that you don't need to go out and buy instant espresso powder or sumac, or a bottle of whiskey, to make one cake if you don't want to! That means that there are some optional ingredients listed here and there. They are mostly little flavor enhancers that you can certainly try the cake without. But if you find yourself baking quite a bit, you might want to grab these enhancers next time you are at the store.

Baking Soda and Baking Powder: These leaveners are what make cakes rise, soft and puffy and golden brown. Baking soda and baking powder have long shelf lives, with an expiration date on the containers, but my personal rule is to replace them every six months or so. There is nothing more frustrating than expired leavening, especially in a cake. Just ask me about the baking workshop I taught in Greece, when all the baking powder had expired, but I didn't figure it out until the last day. Don't be me!

If you haven't used your baking soda or baking powder in a while, you can test the freshness with the following methods:

TEST YOUR BAKING SODA by stirring about 1 teaspoon into ¼ cup white vinegar; it should bubble and fizz like an elementary-school science-fair volcano.

TEST YOUR BAKING POWDER by putting 1 teaspoon into a heat-safe container and pouring about ¼ cup boiling water on top; if it bubbles and fizzes, you are good to go.

Butter: These recipes use standard American grocery-store butter, which has at least 80 percent butterfat. European-style butter starts at 82 percent and can be up to 85 percent butterfat, so while it is richer, it might make your cake a little flat and oily. The cakes that call for butter use melted butter, and it should be slightly warm to the touch but not super hot.

how to brown butter

Some recipes call for browned butter, which adds a toasty, nutty flavor and enhances everything it touches, especially the cozy spice cakes and fruit cakes.

To brown butter, melt the butter in a small saucepan or skillet with a light-colored interior over medium heat; use a light-colored pan so you can see the milk solids change color from white to toasty brown. I like to use a ceramic nonstick skillet because the toasted milk solids slide easily right out of the pan; you may have to scrape a bit if you use a pan that does not have a nonstick coating.

Cook the butter, stirring occasionally, scraping the bits off the bottom and sides of the pan if necessary, for about 3 minutes, until the butter solids turn golden brown and the butter smells nutty. The butter will continue to cook if you leave it in the pan, even if you take it off the heat, so it's a good idea to have a heat-safe bowl close by and transfer the butter so it doesn't burn. Let the butter cool slightly while you grab the rest of the ingredients for your cake. Any time a recipe calls for melted butter, feel free to brown it first.

Buttermilk: Buttermilk adds tang and tenderness to cakes, and it's one of my back-pocket tricks for making cakes extra tasty. It also lasts a long, long time in your fridge, and since you're bound to be baking lots of snack cakes in the near future, go ahead and pick up a container of the real stuff. In a pinch, you can mix 2 parts plain yogurt with 1 part milk and substitute that for the buttermilk in a recipe, just don't do that milk + vinegar or lemon juice thing. It doesn't work that well for these cakes.

Chocolate: Most of the time I prefer chopped chocolate bars over chocolate chips, but I do love the convenience (and appearance) of a preformed little chip every once in a while, so you'll see both appear in the recipes. When a recipe calls for only chopped chocolate, don't substitute chips. The chips contain stabilizers that will affect the finished texture of your bakes. However, in many cases either is just fine, and the ingredients list will include both as options.

Cocoa Powder: These recipes call for unsweetened Dutch-process cocoa, which is cocoa that has been processed with alkali, making it darker in color and deeper in flavor. Dutch-process cocoa also dissolves more readily in liquid, which is ideal for these quick cakes.

Confectioners' Sugar: Confectioners' sugar is the base for most of the delicious glaze and frosting recipes. Conventional and organic confectioners' sugar can be used interchangeably, but they are slightly different. Conventional confectioners' sugar is bright white and usually has cornstarch added as an anti-caking agent. The organic type is made from less processed sugar so it is usually a bit creamier in color and sometimes uses tapioca starch instead of cornstarch as the anti-caking agent.

Start slowly when you add liquid to your confectioners' sugar–based glazes, as you might not need all of it, and feel free to add a drop or two more to make the glaze your preferred consistency. With either, just adjust the liquid to get a thick but pourable glaze for the best coverage.

Eggs: Eggs provide structure, moisture, and lift to the cakes. In these recipes, always use large eggs, and you can use them straight from the fridge.

Flour: Most of these recipes use plain old all-purpose flour. I reach for an unbleached variety, and usually I choose one that is lower in protein, like Gold Medal or Pillsbury. I also love using whole-grain flours in my baking, so you'll see those flours sprinkled in here and there. A bit of whole wheat, buckwheat, or rye flour can transform a simple cake into something truly craveable.

If you aren't the type to keep your pantry stocked with lots of flours, I get it! Rather than committing to a whole bag of flour, check your local supermarket or natural foods shop for bulk bins, where you can pick up a small amount of a new-to-you flour and give it a try. If you don't feel like doing that, just substitute an equal amount of all-purpose flour for the whole grain. But I really encourage you to try a little whole-grain flour in your baking. It is so tasty.

Are you gluten-free? There is a great Citrusy Almond Cornmeal Cake (page 98) that is naturally gluten-free, and I have had good luck using the 1-for-1 gluten-free flour blends that are on the market these days.

Freeze-Dried Fruit: Freeze-dried fruits are more available than ever, and they are flavor powerhouses. You can use them to flavor and naturally tint your glazes and frostings, or to add a bit of crunchy, tasty decoration on top of your cakes. Freeze-dried berries are my favorite, but you can also find freeze-dried pineapple, mango, and many others. Give them a try!

Instant Espresso Powder: This little flavor bomb is one of my favorite baking ingredients. It makes chocolate taste more chocolatey, its bitter edge can temper the sweetness of caramel, and it's a nice little note to add to spice cakes and gingerbread. If you buy one specialty item to up your cake game, this should be it!

Milk: Whole milk is preferred in these cake recipes, but 2% or skim can be used if that's what you keep in your fridge—use what you have! Glaze or icing recipes will be a bit less opaque and rich (and tasty) if you use milk with a lower fat percentage. Unsweetened nondairy milk can also be used in a pinch for our dairy-free friends.

Neutral Oil: "What the heck is neutral oil?" you ask. Well, it's an oil that's odorless and flavorless, so it won't affect the flavor of your cakes, but it will add moisture and give your cakes a lovely soft texture. I recommend canola or grapeseed oil; avocado oil is also a good option but a little pricier.

Nut and Seed Butters: I love spreading natural peanut butter on toast, but for the recipes that call for smooth peanut butter, use sweetened, commercially made peanut butter. I like Smooth Operator, made by Peanut Butter and Co., and the classic Skippy. Recipes that call for natural almond butter or peanut butter should be made with their oilier, unsweetened counterparts—just make sure to stir in the oil that collects on the top before you do the measuring. Same goes for tahini—make sure to stir in the oil that collects on the top before measuring.

Nuts: Most of the time nuts just taste better if they are lightly toasted, which is why pretty much all these recipes call for

toasted nuts. My preferred method is to spread nuts in a single layer on a baking sheet, then pop them into the oven while it is preheating and take them out when they are golden and fragrant, about 10 minutes. The timing depends a little bit on how fast your oven heats; you may want to start checking at 5 minutes.

One recipe calls for adding the nuts to a skillet of melting butter to toast them, and honestly, how could you argue with butter-toasted nuts?

Olive Oil: Some of these cakes call for olive oil, and that's because olive oil is delicious! It also pairs well with chocolate, citrus, and other fruits. Use a flavorful, fruity olive oil rather than a grassy oil, if possible.

Salt: Salt is a tricky topic in cooking and baking these days. I always use Diamond Crystal kosher salt for cooking and baking, which is a bit less salty by volume than fine sea salt, Morton's kosher salt, or table salt. So, these recipes were written with Diamond Crystal in mind. If you aren't able to find Diamond Crystal and you use one of the other salts listed here, you'll want to use a scant measurement of salt or you will find the cake to be salty.

Spices: Do your spice cakes taste bland and boring? Old spices may be the culprit. For the best flavor, use your spices within about six months of purchase. If you don't bake a lot, or you don't have space to store lots of spice jars, check if your local supermarket or natural foods store sells bulk spices so that you can just pick up what you need in the short term.

Spirits: Rum, whiskey, and flavored liqueurs are a great way to add a little bit of concentrated flavor to these simple cakes, but don't worry if you don't keep your home bar stocked. You can purchase tiny airplane-serving-size bottles, or just skip it altogether.

Sugar: White, light brown, dark brown, and turbinado sugars all have a place in these recipes. Turbinado and demerara sugars can be used interchangeably anytime I call for coarse sugar to sprinkle on top of a cake, like my favorite Sparkling Gingerbread (page 123).

Vanilla Bean Paste and Vanilla Extract: These two flavorings are real workhorses in any baking pantry. Fruit, chocolate, spices, and nuts all pair well with floral, sweet vanilla, so you'll find it in quite a few recipes. These two products can be used interchangeably, so no stress if you don't keep both stocked. The little flecks of vanilla beans in vanilla bean paste are quite lovely though, so I use vanilla bean paste when I know they can take center stage, as in the Fluffy Vanilla Frosting (page 173).

Yogurt: There are two types of yogurt used in these recipes—Greek and plain full-fat yogurt. They are not interchangeable. Greek yogurt, which is full-fat yogurt that has been strained, behaves more like super-tart sour cream than the plain full-fat yogurt. Follow the recipe here, as substituting one for the other can make cakes a little spongy.

Zest: When a recipe calls for citrus zest, you can just zest the fruit right into the bowl along with the eggs and sugar. Zesting the fruit directly into the bowl captures all the delicious, flavorful citrus oils that would otherwise be left behind on your countertop or cutting board.

Whisking the zest with the sugar and eggs also breaks up the zest pieces and distributes the flavor evenly through the mixture. As a general rule, one small orange or grapefruit, or two lemons, limes, or tangerines, makes about 1 tablespoon of finely grated zest.

fruit
cakes

fruit cakes are my first love. I grew up in the Pacific Northwest, where some of the most delicious fruit in the entire country grows. So, when I want to bake, I almost always choose something fruity. Folding a bit of fruit into cake batter adds color, texture, and pops of tasty goodness. Fruit purees like applesauce or pumpkin add wonderful moisture. Fruit also pairs nicely with citrus, spice, and chocolate.

Most of these cakes use fruit that is available just about any time of year, but think seasonally when you are preparing to bake. Apples and pears are best in the fall, berries are best in the spring and summer, and citrus is great year-round, but the most exciting varieties, like Meyer lemons and blood oranges, are in season during the winter months.

Use Another Pan

LOAF: Fold ¾ cup (120g) berries into the batter and sprinkle ¼ cup (40g) over the top. Bake the cake in a 9 x 5 x 3-inch loaf pan until puffed and golden, and a skewer inserted into the center comes out clean, 50 to 60 minutes.

ROUND: Bake in a 9-inch round pan until puffed and golden, and a tester inserted into the center comes out clean, 35 to 45 minutes.

Dress It Up

Top this cake with dollops of Fresh Berry Whip (page 181) or Crème Fraîche Whip (page 180).

Flavor Variations

CRANBERRY CREAM CHEESE CAKE: Substitute 1 cup (100g) fresh or frozen whole cranberries for the mixed berries. Fold half into the batter and sprinkle half on top.

APRICOT AND BERRY CREAM CHEESE CAKE: Substitute a combination of 1 cup (170g) sliced apricots and ½ cup (80g) berries for the mixed berries.

Berry Cream Cheese Cake

This berry and cream cheese combination is inspired by the genius cream cheese–studded muffins at Sister Pie, a bakery started by Lisa Ludwinski in Detroit. I like a combination of blueberries and raspberries, but you can add blackberries, too. Strawberries get a little too soft when they are folded into this batter, so save them for the Whole-Grain Strawberry Cake (page 79).

¾ cup (150g) dark brown sugar

2 large eggs

¾ cup (165g) sour cream

½ cup (113g) unsalted butter, melted

1 teaspoon vanilla extract

¾ teaspoon kosher salt

1½ cups (190g) all-purpose flour

1½ teaspoons baking powder

½ teaspoon baking soda

¼ cup (70g) cream cheese, cold

1 cup (160g) mixed fresh berries

1 tablespoon turbinado sugar

1. Position a rack in the center of your oven and preheat the oven to 350°F. Butter or coat an 8-inch square baking pan with nonstick spray. Line the pan with a strip of parchment paper that hangs over two of the edges.

2. In a large bowl, whisk the brown sugar and eggs until pale and foamy, about 1 minute. Add the sour cream, butter, vanilla, and salt. Whisk until smooth and emulsified.

3. Add the flour, baking powder, and baking soda to the bowl. Whisk until well-combined and smooth.

4. Use your fingers to break up the cream cheese into teaspoon-size pieces and scatter them over the top of the batter. Fold in the cream cheese and ½ cup (80g) of the berries.

5. Pour the batter into the prepared pan, tap the pan gently on the counter to release any air bubbles, and smooth the top of the batter with an offset spatula. Scatter the remaining berries over the top and sprinkle with the turbinado sugar.

6. Bake the cake until puffed and golden, and a tester inserted into the center comes out clean, 30 to 45 minutes. Set the cake on a rack to cool for about 15 minutes. Then use the parchment paper to lift the cake out of the pan and set it on the rack to cool completely. Serve warm or at room temperature. (Store the cake, wrapped tightly, in the fridge, for up to three days.)

Black- and Blueberry Ricotta Cake

This deceptively simple ricotta cake is perfectly light and fluffy, and it couldn't be easier to make. Here, I've folded in a combination of sweet and tart blueberries and blackberries, but just about any other fruit or even a bit of chocolate would work beautifully.

¾ cup (150g) plus 2 teaspoons sugar

2 large eggs

1 cup (220g) whole-milk ricotta

½ cup (120ml) neutral oil, like canola or grapeseed

1 teaspoon vanilla extract

¾ teaspoon kosher salt

1¼ cups (160g) all-purpose flour

1½ teaspoons baking powder

½ teaspoon baking soda

1½ cups (240g) mixed blackberries and blueberries

1. Position a rack in the center of your oven and preheat the oven to 350°F. Butter or coat an 8-inch square baking pan with nonstick spray. Line the pan with a strip of parchment paper that hangs over two of the edges.

2. In a large bowl, whisk ¾ cup (150g) of the sugar and the eggs until pale and foamy, about 1 minute. Add the ricotta, oil, vanilla, and salt. Whisk until smooth and emulsified.

3. Add the flour, baking powder, and baking soda and stir until well-combined and smooth, making sure to scrape the bottom and sides of the bowl. Use a rubber spatula to fold in 1 cup (160g) of the berries, reserving the remaining berries to sprinkle over the top.

4. Pour the batter into the prepared pan, tap the pan gently on the counter to release any air bubbles, and smooth the top of the batter with an offset spatula. Scatter the reserved ½ cup (80g) berries over the top and sprinkle with the remaining 2 teaspoons sugar.

5. Bake the cake until puffed and golden, and a tester inserted into the center comes out clean, 40 to 50 minutes. Set the pan on a rack to cool for about 15 minutes. Then use the parchment paper to lift the cake out of the pan and set it on the rack to cool completely. (Store the cake, wrapped tightly, at room temperature or in the fridge, for up to three days.)

Use Another Pan

LOAF: Fold ¾ cup (120g) berries into the batter and sprinkle ¼ cup (40g) over the top. Bake in a 9 x 5 x 3-inch loaf pan until puffed and golden, and a skewer inserted into the center comes out clean, 55 to 65 minutes.

ROUND: Bake in a 9-inch round pan until puffed and golden, and a tester inserted into the center comes out clean, 40 to 50 minutes.

Flavor Variations

ZESTY RICOTTA CAKE: Zest 1 lemon or lime directly into the bowl before you add the sugar and eggs, substitute an equal amount of olive oil for the neutral oil, and then top the cooled cake with Lemon Glaze (page 44).

STONE-FRUIT RICOTTA CAKE: Try the cake with chopped stone fruit instead of blueberries and blackberries. Plums or nectarines would be delicious.

BERRY RICOTTA CORN CAKE: Fold in ½ cup (50g) of the freshest, sweetest summer corn kernels (uncooked) you can find along with the berries. Seriously, only use supersweet corn here.

Dress It Up

Serve slices of cake with dollops of Vanilla Bean Whip (page 182) or with ice cream and fresh fruit.

Use Another Pan

BUNDT: Double the ingredients for the cake and bake in a prepared 15-cup Bundt pan until puffed and golden, and a skewer inserted into the center comes out clean, 50 to 60 minutes. Let the cake cool in the pan for 15 minutes, then invert onto a rack to cool completely.

LOAF: Bake in a 9 x 5 x 3-inch loaf pan until puffed and golden, and a skewer inserted into the center comes out clean, 50 to 60 minutes.

ROUND: Bake in a 9-inch round pan until puffed and golden, and a tester inserted into the center comes out clean, 35 to 45 minutes.

Flavor Variations

MAPLE BANANA CAKE: Prepare the cake as directed, then top with Maple Coffee Glaze (page 91).

TAHINI BANANA CAKE: Prepare the cake as directed, then top with Tahini Glaze (page 116).

Dress It Up

Serve warm slices of cake with scoops of vanilla ice cream and warm Whiskey Caramel (page 126) drizzled over the top.

Buckwheat Banana Cake

Supersweet bananas can stand up to a bit of whole-grain flour, and in this cake buckwheat flour adds a little wholesome flair. You can also use whole wheat flour in place of the buckwheat, and if you don't keep whole-grain flours handy, just go ahead and use all-purpose. You'll be happy any way you slice it.

½ cup (100g) sugar

2 large eggs

1 cup (230g) mashed very ripe banana (about 2 bananas)

½ cup (110g) plain full-fat Greek yogurt

1 teaspoon vanilla extract

¾ teaspoon kosher salt

1 cup (128g) all-purpose flour

½ cup (65g) buckwheat or whole wheat flour

¾ teaspoon baking soda

½ cup (113g) unsalted butter, melted

1. Position a rack in the center of your oven and preheat the oven to 350°F. Butter or coat an 8-inch square baking pan with nonstick spray. Line the pan with a strip of parchment paper that hangs over two of the edges.

2. In a large bowl, whisk the sugar and eggs until pale and foamy, about 1 minute. Add the mashed banana, yogurt, vanilla, and salt and whisk until smooth and emulsified.

3. Add the all-purpose flour, buckwheat flour, and baking soda and use a rubber spatula to stir until well-combined and smooth. Fold in the butter, making sure to scrape the sides and bottom of the bowl.

4. Pour the batter into the prepared pan, tap the pan gently on the counter to release any air bubbles, and smooth the top of the batter with an offset spatula.

5. Bake the cake until puffed and golden, and a tester inserted into the center comes out clean, 35 to 45 minutes. Set the pan on a rack to cool for about 15 minutes. Then use the parchment paper to lift the cake out of the pan and set it on the rack to cool completely.

Buttery Brown Sugar Pear and Cranberry Cake

I like Comice or Bartlett pears in this cake because they are soft and sweet, but not too soft to hold their own in the buttery batter. Aim for pear pieces that are about the size of the cranberries, but no need to get out a ruler. The chopped hazelnuts echo the toasty notes in the browned butter, so don't skip 'em.

½ cup (113g) unsalted butter

½ cup (100g) light brown sugar

¼ cup (60ml) maple syrup

2 large eggs

½ cup (110g) sour cream

1 teaspoon vanilla extract

½ teaspoon kosher salt

A few grates of nutmeg

1¼ cups (160g) all-purpose flour

1½ teaspoons baking powder

¼ teaspoon baking soda

1 cup (150g) chopped peeled pear

1 cup (100g) fresh or frozen cranberries

½ cup (65g) chopped hazelnuts

1 tablespoon turbinado sugar

1. Position a rack in the center of your oven and preheat the oven to 350°F. Butter or coat an 8-inch square baking pan with nonstick spray. Line the pan with a strip of parchment paper that hangs over two of the edges.

2. **BROWN THE BUTTER:** Melt the butter in a small saucepan or skillet with a light-colored interior over medium heat. Cook the butter for about 3 minutes, stirring occasionally, scraping the bits up from the bottom and sides of the pan, if necessary, until the butter solids turn golden brown and smell nutty. Pour the butter into a large heatproof bowl and let cool slightly.

3. Add the brown sugar, maple syrup, and eggs to the warm butter and whisk until well-combined and smooth. Add the sour cream, vanilla, salt, and nutmeg. Whisk until smooth and emulsified.

4. Add the flour, baking powder, and baking soda and whisk until well-combined and smooth. Use a rubber spatula to fold in the pear and cranberries.

5. Pour the batter into the pan, tap the pan gently on the counter to release any air bubbles, and smooth the top of the batter with an offset spatula. Sprinkle the hazelnuts over the batter. Finally, sprinkle the turbinado sugar over the top.

6. Bake the cake until puffed and golden, and a tester inserted into the center comes out clean, 35 to 45 minutes. There might be a bit of moisture on the tester from the fruit. Set the pan on a rack to cool for about 15 minutes. Then use the parchment paper to lift the cake out of the pan and set it on the rack to cool completely. (Store the cake, wrapped tightly, at room temperature for up to two days.)

Use Another Pan

ROUND: Bake in a 9-inch round pan until puffed and golden, and a tester inserted into the center comes out clean, 35 to 45 minutes.

LOAF: Sprinkle the batter with ¼ cup (32g) chopped hazelnuts instead of ½ cup. Bake the cake in a 9 x 5 x 3-inch loaf pan until puffed and golden, and a skewer inserted into the center comes out clean, 55 to 65 minutes.

SHEET: Double the ingredients and bake in a 9 x 13-inch pan until puffed and golden, and a tester inserted into the center comes out clean, 40 to 50 minutes.

Flavor Variations

APPLE AND CRANBERRY CAKE: Substitute 1 cup (150g) chopped peeled apple for the pear and ½ cup (65g) chopped walnuts for the hazelnuts.

BUTTERY BROWN SUGAR BERRY CAKE: Substitute 1½ cups (240g) mixed blackberries, blueberries, and raspberries for the pear and cranberries. Fold 1 cup (160g) of the berries into the cake, and sprinkle the remaining ½ cup (80g) of them on top before adding the nuts and turbinado sugar.

Dress It Up

Serve slices of cake with scoops of honey or caramel ice cream and a drizzle of warm Whiskey Caramel (page 126).

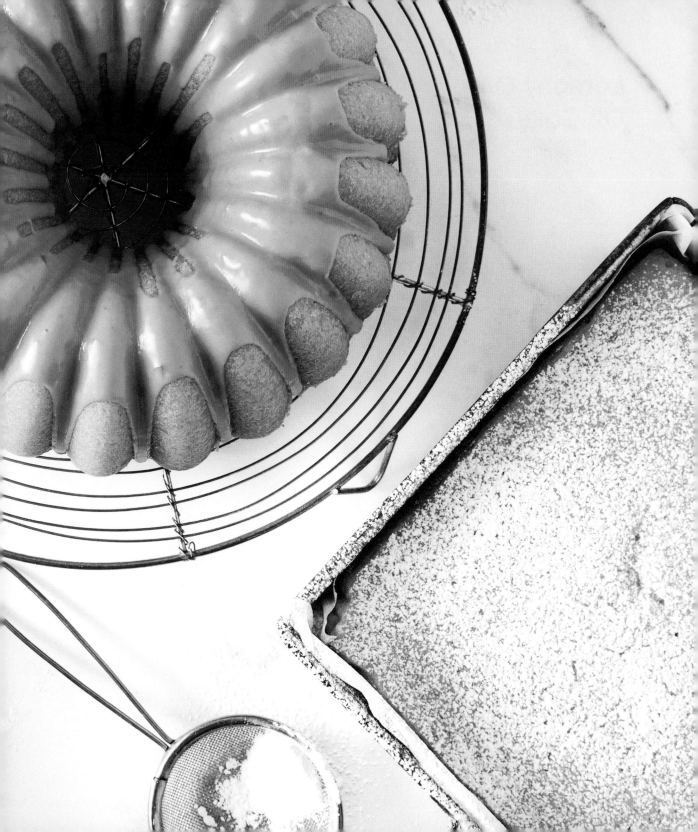

Lemony Olive Oil Cake

This cake highlights bright lemons, but olive oil pairs so nicely with citrus that you can use any citrus you like for the cake and glaze—lime, Meyer lemon, tangerine, blood orange, or grapefruit. You can even combine a few types. I love the combination of the pleasant bitterness and rosy color from pink grapefruit and the sweet, slightly floral scent of Meyer lemons. You'll need about three lemons or limes, two small oranges, or two small grapefruits to yield the 2 tablespoons plus 1 teaspoon of zest necessary for the cake and the glaze.

Lemony Olive Oil Cake

3 lemons

¾ cup (150g) sugar

2 large eggs

1 cup (240ml) buttermilk, well shaken

¾ cup (180ml) olive oil

2 tablespoons Grand Marnier or lemon juice

¾ teaspoon kosher salt

1½ cups (190g) all-purpose flour

1½ teaspoons baking powder

¼ teaspoon baking soda

Lemon Glaze

1 lemon

1 cup (100g) confectioners' sugar

Pinch of salt

1. Position a rack in the center of your oven and preheat the oven to 350°F. Butter or coat an 8-inch square baking pan with nonstick spray. Line the pan with a strip of parchment paper that hangs over two of the edges.

2. **MAKE THE CAKE:** Zest the lemons directly into a large bowl—you're looking for about 2 tablespoons of zest. Add the sugar and eggs and whisk until pale and foamy, about 1 minute. Add the buttermilk, oil, Grand Marnier or lemon juice, and salt. Whisk until smooth and emulsified.

3. Add the flour, baking powder, and baking soda and whisk until well-combined and smooth.

4. Pour the batter into the prepared pan, tap the pan gently on the counter to release any air bubbles, and smooth the top of the batter with an offset spatula.

5. Bake the cake until puffed and golden, and a tester inserted into the center comes out clean, 30 to 40 minutes. Set the pan on a rack to cool for about 15 minutes. Then use the parchment paper to lift the cake out of the pan and set it on the rack to cool completely.

6. **MAKE THE GLAZE:** Zest about 1 teaspoon of lemon zest into a bowl. Juice the lemon and measure 1 tablespoon of juice. Add the confectioners' sugar, 1 tablespoon lemon juice, and salt to the bowl with the zest. Whisk until smooth. If necessary, add more lemon juice, 1 teaspoon at a time, to make a thick but pourable glaze.

7. Pour the glaze over the cooled cake and let set for about 20 minutes before slicing the cake. (Store the cake, covered, at room temperature for up to three days. The glaze will soften over time.)

Use Another Pan

BUNDT: Double the ingredients for the cake and bake in a prepared 15-cup Bundt pan until puffed and golden, and a skewer inserted into the center comes out clean, 45 to 55 minutes. Let the cake cool in the pan for 10 minutes, then invert onto a rack to cool completely. Double the ingredients for the glaze, too.

LOAF: Bake in a 9 x 5 x 3-inch loaf pan until puffed and golden, and a skewer inserted into the center comes out clean, 45 to 55 minutes. You'll need a half batch of glaze to coat the cake in a thin layer.

ROUND: Bake in a 9-inch round pan until puffed and golden, and a tester inserted into the center comes out clean, 35 to 45 minutes.

Flavor Variations

CHOOSE-YOUR-OWN-ADVENTURE OLIVE OIL CAKE: Substitute any other citrus (or a combination!) for the lemons, and don't worry about getting exactly 2 tablespoons of zest—a little more or less is totally okay.

CITRUS-SOAKED OLIVE OIL CAKE: Skip the glaze and prepare a batch of Citrus Syrup (page 98). Pour the syrup over the warm cake while it is cooling in the pan. Let it sit for at least 1 hour before slicing. If the cake is a Bundt, pour the syrup over the cake just after you unmold it onto the rack, while it's still warm.

STRAWBERRY AND APEROL CITRUS OLIVE OIL CAKE: Make a strawberry Aperol glaze by whisking 1¼ cups (125g) confectioners' sugar, 2 tablespoons crushed fresh strawberries, 1 tablespoon Aperol, and a pinch of salt in a small bowl. Pour it over the cooled cake and serve with more strawberries.

OLIVE OIL YOGURT CAKE: Replace the buttermilk with 1 cup (220g) plain whole-milk yogurt.

Dress It Up

Serve this cake with fresh fruit and Honey Whip (page 181) or Fresh Berry Whip (page 181).

Coconut Lime Cake

This cake is packed with coconut milk, coconut oil, and shredded coconut for maximum coconut flavor. If the cream is separated from your coconut milk, make sure to whisk it until it's emulsified before measuring. Eat this cake while dreaming that you are somewhere warm, sipping a drink with an umbrella and an obscenely huge fruit garnish sticking out of the top.

Coconut Lime Cake

1 lime

¾ cup (150g) sugar

2 large eggs

¾ cup (180ml) full-fat coconut milk, well stirred

½ cup (120ml) coconut oil, melted

½ teaspoon kosher salt

1¼ cups (160g) all-purpose flour

⅓ cup (32g) unsweetened shredded coconut

1½ teaspoons baking powder

½ teaspoon baking soda

Coconut Lime Glaze

1 lime

1 cup (100g) confectioners' sugar

2 to 3 tablespoons full-fat coconut milk, well stirred, or more as needed

½ cup (50g) unsweetened flaked or shredded coconut, toasted

Pinch of salt

1. Position a rack in the center of your oven and preheat the oven to 350°F. Butter or coat an 8-inch square baking pan with nonstick spray. Line the pan with a strip of parchment paper that hangs over two of the edges.

2. **MAKE THE CAKE:** Zest the lime directly into a large bowl and add the sugar and eggs. Whisk until pale and foamy, about 1 minute. Add the coconut milk, coconut oil, and salt. Whisk until smooth and emulsified.

3. Add the flour, coconut, baking powder, and baking soda. Whisk until well-combined and smooth.

4. Pour the batter into the prepared pan, tap the pan gently on the counter to release any air bubbles, and smooth the top of the batter with an offset spatula.

5. Bake the cake until puffed and golden, and a tester inserted into the center comes out clean, 30 to 40 minutes. Set the pan on a rack to cool for about 15 minutes. Then use the parchment paper to lift the cake out of the pan and set it on the rack to cool completely.

6. **MAKE THE GLAZE:** Zest about 1 teaspoon lime zest into a bowl. Add the confectioners' sugar and 2 tablespoons coconut milk and whisk until smooth. Add a bit more coconut milk as necessary to make a thick, pourable glaze.

7. Pour the glaze over the cooled cake and gently help it spread a bit. Top the glaze with the toasted coconut and, if desired, additional lime zest. Let the glaze set for about 20 minutes before slicing the cake. (Store the cake, covered, at room temperature for up to three days. The glaze will soften over time.)

Flavor Variations

CHOCOLATE COCONUT CAKE: Omit the lime zest and substitute ¼ cup (23g) unsweetened cocoa powder for ¼ cup (32g) of the flour. Glaze the cooled cake with Cocoa Glaze (page 135) and top with toasted coconut.

COCONUT LEMON CAKE: Substitute lemon for the lime in the cake and the glaze.

→ Use Another Pan

BUNDT: Double the ingredients for the cake and bake in a prepared 15-cup Bundt pan until puffed and golden, and a skewer inserted into the center comes out clean, 45 to 55 minutes. Let the cake cool in the pan for 10 minutes, then invert onto a rack to cool completely. Double the ingredients for the glaze, too.

LOAF: Bake the cake in a 9 x 5 x 3-inch loaf pan until puffed and golden, and a skewer inserted into the center comes out clean, 40 to 50 minutes. You'll need a half batch of glaze to coat the cake in a thin layer.

Dress It Up

Top the cake with Vanilla Bean Whip (page 182) and some maraschino cherries. Okay, the cherries aren't necessary, but they are fun!

Use Another Pan

ROUND: Bake in a 9-inch round pan until puffed and golden, and a tester inserted into the center comes out clean, 35 to 45 minutes.

Flavor Variations

BERRY COCONUT ALMOND CAKE: Add the zest of 1 lemon to the sugar and eggs when you whisk them together. Substitute thinly sliced strawberries or any other berry for the cherries.

Dress It Up

Add dollops of Crème Fraîche Whip (page 180) or scoops of ice cream to warm slices of cake and you'll be very, very happy.

Cherry Coconut Almond Cake

Coconut and almond are a match made in nutty heaven, and they pair as nicely with each other as just about any fruit you can imagine. If you can find sour cherries, they are delicious in this recipe, but sweet cherries are just as good. An extra sprinkle of almonds, coconut, and sugar gives this cake a crispy and toothsome top.

¾ cup (150g) plus 1½ teaspoons sugar

2 large eggs

1 cup (240ml) buttermilk, well shaken

½ cup (120ml) liquid coconut oil or neutral oil, like canola or grapeseed

1 teaspoon vanilla extract

½ teaspoon coconut extract (optional)

¾ teaspoon kosher salt

1 cup (128g) all-purpose flour

½ cup (55g) almond flour

½ cup (40g) plus 1 tablespoon unsweetened shredded coconut

2 teaspoons baking powder

1 cup (140g) halved cherries, fresh or frozen

2 tablespoons sliced almonds or chopped almonds (optional)

1. Position a rack in the center of your oven and preheat the oven to 350°F. Butter or coat an 8-inch square pan with nonstick spray. Line the pan with a strip of parchment paper that hangs over two of the edges.

2. In a large bowl, whisk ¾ cup (150g) of the sugar and the eggs until pale and foamy, about 1 minute. Add the buttermilk, oil, vanilla, coconut extract (if using), and salt. Whisk until smooth and emulsified.

3. Add the all-purpose flour, almond flour, ½ cup (40g) of the coconut, and the baking powder. Whisk until well-combined and smooth.

4. Pour the batter into the prepared pan and tap the pan gently on the counter to release any air bubbles. Scatter the cherries in an even layer over the top of the batter, then scatter the remaining tablespoon coconut, the almonds (if using), and the remaining 1½ teaspoons sugar over the cherries.

5. Bake the cake until puffed and golden, and a tester inserted into the center comes out clean, 35 to 45 minutes. There may be a bit of moisture on the tester from the cherries. Set the pan on a rack to cool for about 15 minutes. Then use the parchment paper to lift the cake out of the pan and set it on the rack to cool completely. (Store the cake, wrapped tightly, at room temperature for up to two days.)

Grapefruit White Chocolate Cake

This cake is all about the balance of sweet and creamy white chocolate and mouth-puckering, slightly bitter grapefruit. Make sure to use the best-quality white chocolate you can find; Valrhona and Cacao Berry both make a few delicious varieties. Choose a pink grapefruit for the prettiest glaze. You'll need two grapefruits to make enough zest for the cake and glaze.

Grapefruit White Chocolate Cake

1 medium grapefruit

¾ cup (150g) sugar

2 large eggs

1 cup (220g) plain whole-milk yogurt

½ cup (120ml) neutral oil, such as canola or grapeseed

1 teaspoon vanilla extract

½ teaspoon kosher salt

1½ cups (190g) all-purpose flour

1½ teaspoons baking powder

¼ teaspoon baking soda

½ cup (85g) chopped white chocolate or white chocolate chips

Grapefruit Glaze

1 medium grapefruit

1 cup (100g) confectioners' sugar

Pinch of salt

1. Position a rack in the center of your oven and preheat the oven to 350°F. Butter or coat an 8-inch square baking pan with nonstick spray. Line the pan with a strip of parchment paper that hangs over two of the edges.

2. **MAKE THE CAKE:** Zest the grapefruit into a large bowl, then juice it and measure ¼ cup (60ml) of juice. Add the sugar and eggs and whisk until pale and foamy, about 1 minute. Add the yogurt, oil, ¼ cup (60ml) grapefruit juice, vanilla, and salt. Whisk until smooth and emulsified.

3. Add the flour, baking powder, and baking soda and whisk until well-combined and smooth. Fold in the white chocolate.

4. Pour the batter into the prepared pan, tap the pan gently on the counter to release any air bubbles, and smooth the top of the batter with an offset spatula.

5. Bake the cake until puffed and golden, and a tester inserted into the center comes out clean, 40 to 50 minutes. Set the pan on a rack to cool for about 15 minutes. Then use the parchment paper to lift the cake out of the pan and set it on the rack to cool completely.

6. **MAKE THE GLAZE:** Zest about 1 teaspoon of grapefruit zest into a bowl. Juice half the grapefruit and measure 1 tablespoon juice. Add the confectioners' sugar, 1 tablespoon grapefruit juice, and the salt to the bowl with the zest. Whisk until smooth. If necessary, add more grapefruit juice, 1 teaspoon at a time, to make a thick but pourable glaze.

7. Pour the glaze over the cooled cake and let set for about 20 minutes before slicing the cake. (Store the cake, covered, at room temperature for up to three days. The glaze will soften over time.)

Use Another Pan

BUNDT: Double the ingredients for the cake and bake in a prepared 15-cup Bundt pan until puffed and golden, and a skewer inserted into the center comes out clean, 50 to 60 minutes. Let the cake cool in the pan for 10 minutes, then invert it onto a rack to cool completely. Double the ingredients for the glaze, too.

LOAF: Bake in a 9 x 5 x 3-inch loaf pan until puffed and golden, and a skewer inserted into the center comes out clean, 55 to 65 minutes. You'll need a half batch of glaze to coat the cake in a thin layer.

ROUND: Bake in a 9-inch round pan until puffed and golden, and a tester inserted into the center comes out clean, 35 to 45 minutes.

Flavor Variations

Substitute lemon or lime juice and zest for the grapefruit.

Dress It Up

Serve slices of cake with ice cream or Whipped Vanilla Mascarpone (page 182) .

Use Another Pan

ROUND: Bake in a 9-inch round pan until puffed and golden, and a tester inserted into the center comes out clean, 30 to 40 minutes. There may be a bit of moisture on the tester from the apples.

LOAF: Bake in a 9 x 5 x 3-inch loaf pan until puffed and golden, and a skewer inserted into the center comes out clean, 45 to 55 minutes. There may be a bit of moisture on the skewer from the apples.

Flavor Variations

MAPLE APPLE CAKE: Top the cooled cake with a drizzle of Maple Coffee Glaze (page 91).

MOSTLY PEACH CAKE: Omit the espresso powder and replace the apples with chopped peeled peaches or nectarines. Since peaches are generally juicier than apples, this cake will soften after about a day. Plan to eat it quickly or store it, well-wrapped, in the refrigerator.

MOSTLY PEARS CAKE: Substitute chopped peeled pears for the apple, and chopped hazelnuts or pecans for the walnuts.

Dress It Up

Serve slices of cake with dollops of Crème Fraîche Whip (page 180).

Mostly Apples Cake

This cake is just what it sounds like—a heap of apples barely held together with a sweet, spicy batter. Make sure you use a tart baking apple that will soften in the oven but still hold its shape. I like Mutsu, Jonathan, and McIntosh. The recipe calls for walnuts, but pecans or hazelnuts would be delicious, too.

¾ cup (150g) dark brown sugar

2 large eggs

⅓ cup (80ml) neutral oil, like canola or grapeseed

1 tablespoon whiskey (optional)

1 teaspoon vanilla extract

1 teaspoon ground cinnamon

¼ teaspoon freshly grated nutmeg

½ teaspoon instant espresso powder (optional)

½ teaspoon kosher salt

1 cup (128g) all-purpose flour

1 teaspoon baking powder

½ teaspoon baking soda

2 small apples, peeled, cored, and chopped into ¼- to ½-inch pieces (about 2 cups)

½ cup (50g) toasted walnuts, chopped

1. Position a rack in the center of your oven and preheat the oven to 350°F. Butter or coat an 8-inch square baking pan with nonstick spray. Line the pan with a strip of parchment paper that hangs over two of the edges.

2. In a large bowl, whisk the brown sugar and eggs until pale and foamy, about 1 minute. Add the oil, whiskey (if using), vanilla, cinnamon, nutmeg, espresso powder (if using), and salt. Whisk until smooth and emulsified.

3. Add the flour, baking powder, and baking soda and whisk until well-combined and smooth.

4. Use a rubber spatula to fold in the apples and ¼ cup (25g) of the nuts.

5. Pour the batter into the prepared pan and use an offset spatula to gently smooth the top, making sure the apples are well dispersed and go all the way to the edges of the pan. Tap the pan gently on the counter to release any air bubbles. Sprinkle the remaining ¼ cup (25g) nuts over the cake.

6. Bake until puffed and golden, and a tester inserted into the center comes out clean, 30 to 40 minutes. There may be a bit of moisture on the tester from the apples. Set the pan on a rack to cool for about 15 minutes. Then use the parchment paper to lift the cake out of the pan and set it on the rack to cool completely. (Store the cake, wrapped tightly, at room temperature or in the fridge for up to two days.)

Nectarine and Cornmeal Upside-Down Cake

Sweet and tart summer nectarines and cornmeal are a natural and delicious pairing. You'll need a small saucepan to melt the butter and sugar together for the topping—hold onto it, because you can melt the butter for the cake in the same pan. You can use peaches here, too, but their skins don't soften quite as much as nectarines do during this cake's short baking time.

Topping

3 tablespoons (42g) unsalted butter

⅓ cup (67g) light brown sugar

Pinch of salt

2 or 3 small nectarines, pitted and cut into ½-inch slices

Cake

1 lemon

½ cup (100g) light brown sugar

2 large eggs

1 cup (220g) whole-milk ricotta

½ cup (113g) unsalted butter, melted

¾ teaspoon kosher salt

1 cup (128g) all-purpose flour

½ cup (65g) finely ground yellow cornmeal

1 teaspoon baking powder

¼ teaspoon baking soda

1. Position a rack in the center of your oven and preheat the oven to 350°F. Butter or coat an 8-inch square baking pan with nonstick spray and line the bottom with a square of parchment paper.

2. **MAKE THE TOPPING:** In a small saucepan, over medium heat, combine the butter, brown sugar, and salt over medium heat. Whisk the mixture occasionally until melted and emulsified, about 3 minutes, then pour into the prepared pan. Tilt the pan to spread the mixture evenly on the bottom of the pan, then arrange the nectarines flat side down in a single layer on top of the caramel. You can arrange them however you like. Follow your heart!

3. **MAKE THE CAKE:** Zest the lemon into a large bowl, then add the brown sugar and eggs and whisk until pale and foamy, about 1 minute. Add the ricotta, butter, and salt. Whisk until smooth and emulsified.

4. Add the flour, cornmeal, baking powder, and baking soda to the bowl. Stir with a rubber spatula until well-combined and smooth. The batter will be quite thick.

5. Spoon the batter over the nectarines in the prepared pan and carefully smooth the top with an offset spatula. Tap the pan a few times on the counter to release any air bubbles and help the batter settle in between the fruit.

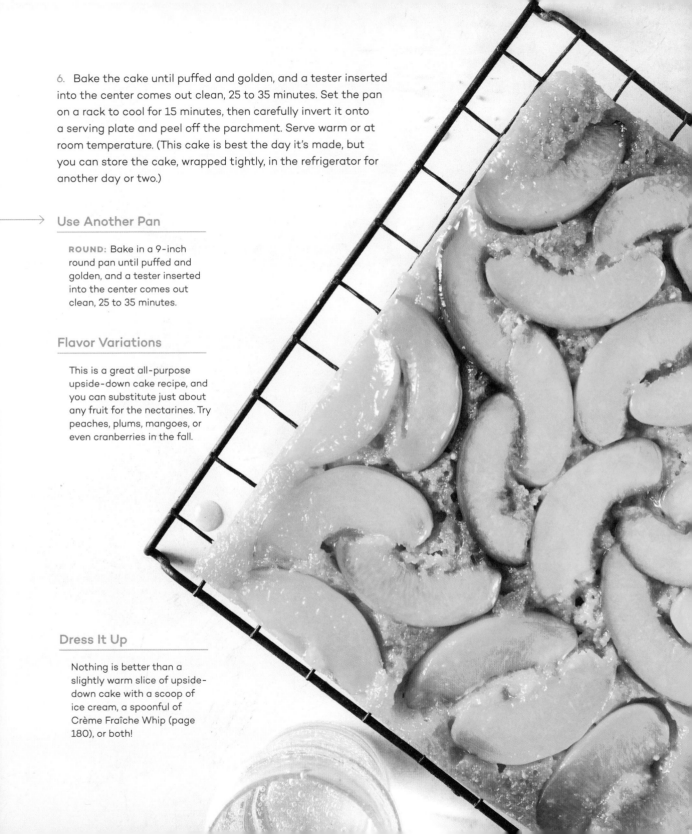

6. Bake the cake until puffed and golden, and a tester inserted into the center comes out clean, 25 to 35 minutes. Set the pan on a rack to cool for 15 minutes, then carefully invert it onto a serving plate and peel off the parchment. Serve warm or at room temperature. (This cake is best the day it's made, but you can store the cake, wrapped tightly, in the refrigerator for another day or two.)

Use Another Pan

ROUND: Bake in a 9-inch round pan until puffed and golden, and a tester inserted into the center comes out clean, 25 to 35 minutes.

Flavor Variations

This is a great all-purpose upside-down cake recipe, and you can substitute just about any fruit for the nectarines. Try peaches, plums, mangoes, or even cranberries in the fall.

Dress It Up

Nothing is better than a slightly warm slice of upside-down cake with a scoop of ice cream, a spoonful of Crème Fraîche Whip (page 180), or both!

Orange-Poppy Seed Cake
with Fresh Raspberry Glaze

I am a sucker for any cake with poppy seeds, but citrus and poppy seeds are a match made in heaven. This super-orangey cake is light and fluffy, and covered with the most beautiful fresh raspberry glaze that couldn't be easier to make. This is a great template for any citrus; see the variations on page 59 for some suggestions.

Orange–Poppy Seed Cake

2 small oranges

½ cup (100g) sugar

2 large eggs

1 cup (220g) plain whole-milk yogurt

½ cup (120ml) neutral oil, like canola or grapeseed

2 tablespoons poppy seeds

¾ teaspoon kosher salt

1¼ cups (160g) all-purpose flour

2 teaspoons baking powder

¼ teaspoon baking soda

Fresh Raspberry Glaze

¼ cup (40g) fresh raspberries

1 cup (100g) confectioners' sugar, or more as needed

Pinch of salt

Orange zest, to finish

2 tablespoons freeze-dried raspberries, to finish

1. Position a rack in the center of your oven and preheat the oven to 350°F. Butter or coat an 8-inch square baking pan with nonstick spray. Line the pan with a strip of parchment paper that hangs over two of the edges.

2. **MAKE THE CAKE:** Zest the oranges into a large bowl. Juice 1 orange and measure ¼ cup (60ml) of juice.

3. Add the sugar and eggs to the bowl with the zest. Whisk until pale and foamy, about 1 minute. Add the yogurt, oil, ¼ cup (60ml) orange juice, poppy seeds, and salt. Whisk until smooth and emulsified.

4. Add the flour, baking powder, and baking soda and whisk until well-combined and completely smooth. Use your whisk to scrape the bottom and sides of the bowl to ensure the batter is evenly mixed.

5. Pour the batter into the prepared pan, tap the pan gently on the counter to release any air bubbles, and smooth the top of the batter with an offset spatula.

recipe continues $\longrightarrow$

6. Bake the cake until puffed and golden, and a tester inserted into the center comes out clean, 30 to 35 minutes. Set the pan on a rack to cool for about 15 minutes. Then use the parchment paper to lift the cake out of the pan and set it on the rack to cool completely.

7. **MAKE THE GLAZE:** Add the raspberries to a medium bowl and use a whisk to crush them. Add the confectioners' sugar and salt. Whisk until smooth. The moisture content in raspberries varies a bit from batch to batch, but the glaze should be quite thick yet pourable. If it's too thin, add a bit more confectioners' sugar. If it's too thick, add a few drops of orange juice or water.

8. Pour the glaze over the cooled cake and sprinkle with a bit of orange zest and, if desired, crushed freeze-dried raspberries. Let the glaze set for about 20 minutes before slicing the cake. Store the cake, wrapped tightly, at room temperature for up to three days. (The freeze-dried raspberries will lose their crunch after the first day.)

Use Another Pan

ROUND: Bake in a 9-inch round pan until puffed and golden, and a tester inserted into the center comes out clean, 30 to 40 minutes.

LOAF: Bake in a 9 x 5 x 3-inch loaf pan until puffed and golden, and a skewer inserted into the center comes out clean, 45 to 55 minutes. You'll need a half batch of glaze to coat the cake in a thin layer.

SHEET: Double the ingredients and bake the cake in a 9 x 13-inch pan until puffed and golden, and a tester inserted into the center comes out clean, 30 to 40 minutes. Double the glaze, too.

Flavor Variations

MEYER LEMON–STRAWBERRY POPPY SEED CAKE: Substitute Meyer lemon zest and juice in the cake for the orange zest and juice and strawberries in the glaze. A perfect spring treat!

DOUBLE-ORANGE POPPY SEED CAKE: Instead of the raspberry glaze, make the Lemon Glaze (page 44), but substitute an equal amount of orange zest and juice for the lemon. Sprinkle a bit of extra orange zest on top, if desired.

Dress It Up

Top slices of glazed or unglazed cake with Fresh Berry Whip (page 181) or Whipped Ricotta with Honey (page 182) and fresh berries.

Rhubarb Crumb Cake
with Sumac Crumb

Rhubarb is my favorite vegetable masquerading as a fruit. It's tart and tangy, and makes my mouth pucker in the best possible way. I love folding rhubarb into all sorts of baked goods, especially cakes topped with a buttery crumb topping. This topping has an unexpected ingredient—dried sumac—which gives it a tart and fruity vibe. If you don't have sumac in your pantry, add about 1 teaspoon of lemon zest instead.

Sumac Crumb

½ cup (63g) all-purpose flour

¼ cup (50g) light brown sugar

¼ cup (23g) old-fashioned rolled oats

2 teaspoons dried sumac

Pinch of salt

¼ cup (55g) unsalted butter, very soft

Rhubarb Cake

1 lemon

¾ cup (150g) light brown sugar

2 large eggs

¾ cup (165g) sour cream

½ cup (113g) unsalted butter, melted

1 teaspoon vanilla bean paste or vanilla extract

½ teaspoon kosher salt

1¼ cups (160g) all-purpose flour

1½ teaspoons baking powder

½ teaspoon baking soda

1½ cups (150g) fresh or frozen chopped rhubarb, in ½-inch pieces

1. Position a rack in the center of your oven and preheat the oven to 350°F. Butter or coat an 8-inch square baking pan with nonstick spray. Line the pan with a strip of parchment paper that hangs over two of the edges.

2. **MAKE THE TOPPING:** Combine the flour, brown sugar, oats, sumac, and salt in a small bowl. Add the butter and smoosh everything together with your fingers until the butter is evenly distributed and crumbs form.

3. **MAKE THE CAKE:** Zest the lemon directly into a large bowl, add the brown sugar and eggs, and whisk until pale and foamy, about 1 minute. Add the sour cream, butter, vanilla, and salt. Whisk until smooth and emulsified.

4. Add the flour, baking powder, and baking soda to the bowl. Whisk until almost combined, then switch to a rubber spatula for the last few strokes; the batter will be quite thick. Fold in the rhubarb.

5. Pour the batter into the prepared pan, tap the pan gently on the counter to release any air bubbles, and smooth the top of the batter with an offset spatula. Then sprinkle the topping over the batter.

6. Bake the cake until puffed and golden, and a tester inserted into the center comes out clean, 50 to 60 minutes. Set the pan on a rack to cool for about 15 minutes. Then use the parchment paper to lift the cake out of the pan and set it on the rack to cool completely. (Store the cake, well wrapped, at room temperature for up to two days.)

Use Another Pan

ROUND: Bake in a 9-inch round pan until puffed and golden, and a tester inserted into the center comes out clean, 50 to 60 minutes.

SKILLET: Bake in a generously buttered 9-inch oven-safe skillet until puffed and golden, and a tester inserted into the center comes out clean, 40 to 50 minutes.

Flavor Variations

BERRY CRUMB CAKE: Substitute an equal amount of fresh berries for the rhubarb—a combination of blueberries and raspberries is especially nice.

Dress It Up

Serve the cake with vanilla ice cream, Brown Sugar Whip (page 180), or Crème Fraîche Whip (page 180) to turn this cake into a satisfying dessert.

Almondy Plum Cake

This cake takes its inspiration from Marian Burros's legendary plum torte recipe, which was first published in the *New York Times* in the 1980s. It's deceptively simple, one of those recipes that is much more than the sum of its parts. Italian plums are my favorite for baking, but any small plums will do.

½ cup (113g) unsalted butter

5 or 6 small plums (about 12 oz./340g)

¾ cup (150g) plus 1 tablespoon sugar

2 large eggs

1 teaspoon vanilla extract

1 teaspoon almond extract (optional)

¾ teaspoon kosher salt

1 cup (128g) all-purpose flour

½ cup (55g) almond flour

1 teaspoon baking powder

3 tablespoons sliced almonds

1. Position a rack in the center of your oven and preheat the oven to 350°F. Butter or coat an 8-inch square baking pan with nonstick spray. Line the pan with a strip of parchment paper that hangs over two of the edges.

2. **BROWN THE BUTTER:** Melt the butter in a small saucepan or skillet with a light-colored interior over medium heat. Cook the butter, stirring occasionally, scraping the bits from the bottom and sides of the pan if necessary, until the butter solids turn golden brown and smell nutty, about 3 minutes. Pour the butter into a large heatproof bowl and let it cool slightly while you prepare the rest of the ingredients.

3. Pit the plums and slice them into quarters while the butter cools a bit.

4. Add ¾ cup (150g) of the sugar and the eggs to the bowl with the warm butter and whisk until pale and foamy, about 1 minute. Add the vanilla, almond extract (if using), and salt. Whisk until smooth and emulsified.

5. Add the all-purpose flour, almond flour, and baking powder and whisk until well-combined and smooth.

6.   Pour the batter into the prepared pan and smooth the top with an offset spatula. Tap the pan gently on the counter to release any air bubbles.

7.   Arrange the plums in snug rows on top of the batter; they should nearly cover the top. Then sprinkle with the sliced almonds and the remaining tablespoon of sugar.

8.   Bake the cake until puffed and golden, and a tester inserted into the center comes out clean, 35 to 45 minutes. Set the pan on a rack to cool for about 15 minutes. Then use the parchment paper to lift the cake out of the pan and set it on the rack to cool completely. Enjoy the cake warm or at room temperature. (Store the cake, wrapped tightly, at room temperature for a day or two or in the fridge for up to three days. I love this cake cold from the fridge.)

Use Another Pan

ROUND: Bake in a 9-inch round pan until puffed and golden, and a tester inserted into the center comes out clean, 35 to 45 minutes.

Flavor Variations

ORANGE BLOSSOM-APRICOT ALMOND CAKE: Add 1 teaspoon orange blossom water when you add the extracts and substitute an equal amount of fresh apricots for the plums.

PERSIMMON ALMOND CAKE: Add the zest of 1 lemon and 1 teaspoon ground ginger with the extracts and substitute an equal amount of peeled Fuyu persimmons for the plums.

Dress It Up

Add a scoop of Crème Fraîche Whip (page 180) or Vanilla Bean Whip (page 182).

Pumpkin Olive Oil Cake
with Maple Olive Oil Glaze

Pumpkin cake isn't just for the fall, and this version, spiked with a bit of allspice and black pepper, has a hit of warmth that makes it more exciting than your average pumpkin spice mix. The glaze has a sweet and savory thing going on that pairs beautifully with the spices. If you prefer your pumpkin cake unadorned, feel free to skip the glaze and just sprinkle a few tablespoons of untoasted pepitas over the top of the cake batter before it goes into the oven.

Pumpkin Olive Oil Cake

1 cup (200g) light brown sugar

2 large eggs

1 cup (230g) pumpkin puree

½ cup (120ml) olive oil

1 teaspoon ground cinnamon

½ teaspoon ground cardamom

⅛ teaspoon ground allspice

A few grinds of black pepper

½ teaspoon kosher salt

1½ cups (190g) all-purpose flour

1 teaspoon baking powder

½ teaspoon baking soda

2 tablespoons chopped toasted pepitas (optional)

1. Position a rack in the center of your oven and preheat the oven to 350°F. Butter or coat an 8-inch square baking pan with nonstick spray. Line the pan with a strip of parchment paper that hangs over two of the edges.

2. **MAKE THE CAKE:** In a large bowl, whisk the brown sugar and eggs until pale and foamy, about 1 minute. Add the pumpkin puree, olive oil, cinnamon, cardamom, allspice, pepper, and kosher salt. Whisk until smooth and emulsified.

3. Add the flour, baking powder, and baking soda and whisk until well-combined and smooth.

4. Pour the batter into the prepared pan, tap the pan gently on the counter to release any air bubbles, and smooth the top of the batter with an offset spatula. Sprinkle the pepitas over the top if you are not going to glaze the cake.

5. Bake until puffed and golden, and a tester inserted into the center comes out clean, 25 to 35 minutes. Set the pan on a rack to cool for about 15 minutes. Then use the parchment paper to lift the cake out of the pan and set it on the rack to cool completely.

Maple Olive Oil Glaze

1 cup (100g) confectioners' sugar

2 tablespoons olive oil

2 tablespoons maple syrup

1 to 2 tablespoons hot water

Pinch of kosher salt

Chopped pepitas (optional)

Flaky salt (optional)

6. **MAKE THE GLAZE:** Combine the confectioners' sugar, olive oil, maple syrup, 1 tablespoon of the hot water, and a pinch of kosher salt in a medium bowl. Whisk until smooth, adding more water as necessary to make a thick but pourable glaze.

7. Pour the glaze over the cooled cake and sprinkle with the pepitas and flaky salt, if desired. Let the glaze set for about 20 minutes before slicing the cake. (Store the cake, well wrapped, at room temperature for up to three days.)

Use Another Pan

LOAF: Bake in a 9 x 5 x 3-inch loaf pan until puffed and golden, and a skewer inserted into the center comes out clean, 50 to 60 minutes. You'll need a half batch of glaze to coat the cake in a thin layer.

ROUND: Bake in a 9-inch round pan until puffed and golden, and a tester inserted into the center comes out clean, 25 to 35 minutes.

SHEET: Double the ingredients for the cake and bake in a 9 x 13-inch pan until puffed and golden, and a tester inserted into the center comes out clean, 30 to 40 minutes. Double the ingredients for the glaze, too.

Dress It Up

Add a dollop of Brown Sugar Whip (page 180) or a scoop of ice cream (or both!) to slices of cake before serving.

Flavor Variations

PUMPKIN CHOCOLATE CHIP CAKE: Prepare the cake as directed, then fold in ½ cup (85g) chopped bittersweet chocolate just before pouring the batter into the pan. Top with Cocoa Glaze (page 135).

RYE PUMPKIN CAKE: Substitute ½ cup (65g) light rye flour for the all-purpose flour. This version is also quite nice with a bit of chocolate folded into the batter.

Swirled Jam Cake

This buttery sour cream cake is a little bit of a choose-your-own adventure. The base is vanilla scented and just sweet enough to highlight your favorite jam. A smooth jam works better here than a chunky preserve, and you can use any flavor you like. I usually choose something in the red berry family. This is the kind of cake you'll definitely want to have for breakfast the next day.

¾ cup (150g) granulated sugar

2 large eggs

1 cup (220g) sour cream

½ cup (113g) unsalted butter, melted

1 teaspoon vanilla bean paste or vanilla extract

¾ teaspoon kosher salt

1½ cups (190g) all-purpose flour

1½ teaspoons baking powder

½ teaspoon baking soda

⅓ cup (80g) smooth jam, any flavor

1 tablespoon confectioners' sugar

1. Position a rack in the center of your oven and preheat the oven to 350°F. Butter or coat an 8-inch square baking pan with nonstick spray. Line the pan with a strip of parchment paper that hangs over two of the edges.

2. In a large bowl, whisk the granulated sugar and eggs until pale and foamy, about 1 minute. Add the sour cream, butter, vanilla, and salt. Whisk until smooth and emulsified.

3. Add the flour, baking powder, and baking soda to the bowl. Whisk until almost combined (the batter will be quite thick), then switch to a rubber spatula for the last few strokes. Make sure to scrape the bottom and sides of the bowl to ensure even mixing.

4. Pour the batter into the prepared pan and tap the pan gently on the counter to release any air bubbles. Dollop the jam in teaspoon-size blobs over the batter, then use a wooden skewer or toothpick to swirl the jam into the batter. This may take a few passes—don't be afraid to get in there and really swirl it around.

5. Bake the cake until puffed and golden, and a tester inserted into the center comes out clean, 35 to 45 minutes. Set the pan on a rack to cool for about 15 minutes. Then use the parchment paper to lift the cake out of the pan and set it on the rack to cool completely. Dust the cooled cake with the confectioners' sugar. (Store the cake, well wrapped, at room temperature for up to three days.)

Use Another Pan

ROUND: Bake in a 9-inch round pan until puffed and golden, and a tester inserted into the center comes out clean, 35 to 45 minutes.

Flavor Variations

BLUEBERRY NUTMEG CAKE: Add the zest of 1 lemon and ½ teaspoon freshly grated nutmeg to the batter when you add the sour cream and vanilla, then swirl with blueberry jam.

PLUM CARDAMOM CAKE: Add the zest of 1 lemon and ½ teaspoon ground cardamom to the batter when you add the sour cream and vanilla, then swirl with plum jam.

Dress It Up

Serve slices of cake with Vanilla Bean Whip (page 182) and fresh fruit.

Spiced Pineapple Upside-Down Cake

I've made a lot of pineapple cakes in my day, and I have finally found the perfect balance of lightly spiced pineapple and soft fluffy cake that is still sturdy enough to soak up all the delicious caramelized juices. I like to slice a fresh pineapple for this cake so I can make thin slices that get meltingly tender during the short baking time.

Topping

3 tablespoons (42g) unsalted butter

⅓ cup (67g) dark brown sugar

1 bay leaf

¼ teaspoon ground cinnamon

A few grinds of black pepper

Pinch of salt

1 tablespoon whiskey or rum (optional)

1 teaspoon vanilla bean paste

1½ cups (225g) thinly sliced pineapple, in 2-inch pieces

Cake

½ cup (100g) dark brown sugar

2 large eggs

1 cup (220g) sour cream

½ cup (120ml) neutral oil, like canola or grapeseed

1 teaspoon vanilla extract

½ teaspoon kosher salt

1½ cups (190g) all-purpose flour

1 teaspoon baking powder

¼ teaspoon baking soda

1. Position a rack in the center of your oven and preheat the oven to 350°F. Butter or coat an 8-inch square pan with nonstick spray. Line the bottom with a square of parchment paper.

2. **MAKE THE TOPPING:** Add the butter, brown sugar, bay leaf, cinnamon, pepper, and salt to a medium skillet. Cook the mixture over medium heat, stirring occasionally, until melted and emulsified. Stir in the whiskey (if using) and vanilla bean paste. Add the pineapple and bring the mixture to a simmer. Cook for about 5 more minutes, turning the pineapple over in the sauce occasionally until it releases its juices and the juices thicken slightly.

3. Remove the bay leaf and carefully pour the mixture into the prepared pan. Use a fork to arrange the pineapple pieces in a single layer.

4. **MAKE THE CAKE:** In a large bowl, whisk the brown sugar and eggs until pale and foamy, about 1 minute. Add the sour cream, oil, vanilla, and salt. Whisk until smooth and emulsified.

5. Add the flour, baking powder, and baking soda to the bowl and whisk until well-combined and smooth. The batter will be thick.

recipe continues ⟶

Use Another Pan

ROUND: Bake the cake in a 9-inch round pan until puffed and golden, and a tester inserted into the center comes out clean, 35 to 45 minutes.

SKILLET: Prepare the pineapple topping in a 9-inch oven-safe skillet, then gently spoon the cake batter over the topping. Bake the cake in the skillet until puffed and golden, and a tester inserted into the center comes out clean, 25 to 35 minutes. Carefully run a thin knife around the edge of the cake, let the cake cool for 10 minutes, then very carefully invert it onto a serving plate. If any pineapple sticks to the pan, just place it right back on top of the cake. No one will know except you.

Dress It Up

Serve slices of cake with ice cream, Crème Fraîche Whip (page 180), or both!

6. Very gently spoon the batter over the pineapple in the prepared pan and smooth the top. Some of the caramel may come up over the sides of the batter. Tuck any pineapple slices that try to sneak up the sides back down into the pan.

7. Bake the cake until puffed and golden, and a tester inserted into the center comes out clean, 30 to 40 minutes. Set the pan on a rack to cool for 10 minutes. Then very carefully invert the cake onto a serving plate. Peel off the parchment paper and serve. (This cake is best the day it's made, but you can store the cake, well wrapped, in the refrigerator for another day or two.)

Strawberry-Glazed Passion Fruit Cake

This punchy combination will bring a little sunshine to the coldest days, and you can make it any time of the year with frozen passion fruit puree and freeze-dried strawberries. Bright, tangy passion fruit puree can be tricky to find, but I have had good luck locating it at my local international grocery in the freezer section. If you can find fresh passion fruit, a few of the seeds sprinkled over the top would make a beautiful, crunchy garnish. If passion fruit isn't available in any form where you live, the strawberry glaze is exceptionally delicious on Lemony Olive Oil Cake (page 44) and Orange–Poppy Seed Cake (page 57).

Passion Fruit Cake

¾ cup (150g) sugar

2 large eggs

½ cup (120ml) passion fruit puree

½ cup (120ml) whole milk

½ cup (120ml) neutral oil, like canola or grapeseed

1 teaspoon vanilla extract

¾ teaspoon kosher salt

1½ cups (190g) all-purpose flour

1½ teaspoons baking powder

¼ teaspoon baking soda

1. Position a rack in the center of your oven and preheat the oven to 350°F. Butter or coat an 8-inch square baking pan with nonstick spray and line with a strip of parchment paper that hangs over two of the edges.

2. **MAKE THE CAKE:** In a large bowl, whisk the sugar and eggs until pale and foamy, about 1 minute. Add the passion fruit puree, milk, oil, vanilla, and salt. Whisk until smooth and emulsified.

3. Add the flour, baking powder, and baking soda to the bowl and whisk until well-combined and smooth.

4. Pour the batter into the prepared pan and tap the pan gently on the counter to release any large air bubbles.

5. Bake the cake until puffed and golden, and a tester inserted into the center comes out clean, 25 to 35 minutes. Set the pan on a rack to cool for about 15 minutes. Then use the parchment paper to lift the cake out of the pan and set it on the rack to cool completely.

recipe and ingrdients continue ⟶

Freeze-Dried Strawberry Glaze

1 cup (100g) confectioners' sugar

¼ cup (7g) freeze-dried strawberries, plus a bit more (optional) for garnish

2 to 3 tablespoons whole milk, or more as needed

Pinch of salt

6. **MAKE THE GLAZE:** Add the confectioners' sugar to a bowl and use your fingers to crumble the strawberries on top. A few small pieces are okay, but you want them to be pretty pulverized. Whisk in 2 tablespoons of the milk and the salt. Add more milk as necessary to make a thick but pourable glaze.

7. Pour the glaze over the cooled cake and spread with a spoon or spatula. Sprinkle a few more crushed freeze-dried strawberries over the top, if desired. Let the glaze set for about 20 minutes before slicing the cake. (Store the cake, covered, at room temperature for up to two days. The freeze-dried berries will soften after the first day.)

Use Another Pan

LOAF: Bake in a 9 x 5 x 3-inch loaf pan until puffed and golden, and a skewer inserted into the center comes out clean, 40 to 45 minutes. You'll need a half batch of glaze to coat the cake in a thin layer.

ROUND: Bake in a 9-inch round pan until puffed and golden, and a tester inserted into the center comes out clean, 25 to 35 minutes.

SHEET: Double the ingredients for the cake and bake in a 9 x 13-inch pan until puffed and golden, and a tester inserted into the center comes out clean, 35 to 45 minutes. Double the glaze, too.

Flavor Variations

This cake is also exceptionally tasty (and a little more festive!) with Fluffy Strawberry Frosting (page 174).

CHOCOLATE PASSION FRUIT CAKE: Passion fruit and chocolate are a delicious combination. Try this cake with Cocoa Glaze (page 135) instead of the strawberry glaze.

Dress It Up

This cake doesn't need much more to make it feel super special, but I like serving slices of cake with dollops of Vanilla Bean Whip (page 182).

Use Another Pan

ROUND: Bake in a 9-inch round pan until puffed and golden, and a tester inserted into the center comes out clean, 45 to 55 minutes.

SKILLET: Bake in a generously buttered 9-inch oven-safe skillet until puffed and golden, and a tester inserted into the center comes out clean, 40 to 50 minutes.

Flavor Variations

STRAWBERRY POPPY SEED CAKE: Stir 2 tablespoons of poppy seeds into the batter along with the flour.

MIXED BERRY CAKE: Substitute any other berry for the strawberries.

Dress It Up

Serve slices of cake with dollops of Vanilla Bean Whip (page 182) and sliced fresh strawberries.

Whole-Grain Strawberry Cake

This is the cake that made me a baked strawberry convert. Normally I find them to be a little soggy, but if you slice the strawberries thin and put them only on top of a cake, they bake into a perfectly sweet, jammy layer. A little bit of whole-grain flour makes all the difference here. You can use whole wheat, spelt, or rye.

1 lemon

¾ cup (150g) plus 2 teaspoons sugar

2 large eggs

¾ cup (165g) plain whole-milk yogurt

½ cup (120ml) neutral oil, like canola or grapeseed

1 teaspoon ground cardamom

1 teaspoon vanilla extract

¾ teaspoon kosher salt

¾ cup (95g) all-purpose flour

½ cup (65g) whole wheat, spelt, or rye flour

1½ teaspoons baking powder

¼ teaspoon baking soda

1¼ cups (140g) hulled and thinly sliced fresh strawberries

1. Position a rack in the center of your oven and preheat the oven to 350°F. Butter or coat an 8-inch square baking pan with nonstick spray. Line the pan with a strip of parchment paper that hangs over two of the edges.

2. Zest the lemon into a large bowl, then add ¾ cup of the sugar and the eggs and whisk until pale and foamy, about 1 minute. Add the yogurt, oil, cardamom, vanilla, and salt. Whisk until smooth and emulsified.

3. Add the all-purpose flour, whole wheat flour, baking powder, and baking soda and stir with a rubber spatula until well-combined and smooth. The batter will be thick.

4. Pour the batter into the prepared pan, tap the pan gently on the counter to release any air bubbles, and smooth the top of the batter with an offset spatula. Scatter the strawberries over the top in a single layer. Or, if you are fastidious, you can arrange the strawberries in neat and tidy rows. Sprinkle the remaining 2 teaspoons sugar over the top.

5. Bake the cake until puffed and deep golden, and a tester inserted into the center comes out clean, 45 to 55 minutes. Set the pan on a rack to cool for about 15 minutes. Then use the parchment paper to lift the cake out of the pan and set it on the rack to cool completely. (Store any leftover cake in the fridge, well wrapped, for a day or two.)

Double Apple Cake

This simple applesauce cake is dressed up with some thinly sliced apples for a presentation befitting a much more complicated recipe. Choose small, tart baking apples for the topping, as you want to be able to fit three rows snugly across the top. If you are lucky enough to find pink-fleshed apples, like Pink Pearls or Mountain Roses, they are exceptionally stunning on this cake.

⅔ cup (133g) light brown sugar

1 large egg

1 cup (250g) unsweetened applesauce

½ cup (120ml) neutral oil, like canola or grapeseed

2 teaspoons ground cinnamon

¼ teaspoon freshly grated nutmeg

⅛ teaspoon ground allspice

½ teaspoon kosher salt

1¼ cups (160g) all-purpose flour

1 teaspoon baking powder

½ teaspoon baking soda

2 small apples (about 300g), peeled, cored, and cut into thin half-moon slices

1 tablespoon granulated or turbinado sugar

Confectioners' sugar, for dusting (optional)

1. Position a rack in the center of your oven and preheat the oven to 350°F. Butter or coat an 8-inch square baking pan with nonstick spray. Line the pan with a strip of parchment paper that hangs over two of the edges.

2. In a large bowl, whisk the brown sugar and egg until pale and foamy, about 2 minutes. Add the applesauce, oil, cinnamon, nutmeg, allspice, and salt. Whisk until smooth and emulsified.

3. Add the flour, baking powder, and baking soda and whisk until well-combined and smooth. Make sure to scrape the sides and bottom of the bowl.

4. Pour the batter into the prepared pan, tap the pan gently on the counter to release any air bubbles, and smooth the top of the batter with an offset spatula. Arrange the apples over the top of the batter in three rows, and sprinkle the granulated sugar over the top.

5. Bake the cake until puffed and golden, and a tester inserted into the center comes out clean, 45 to 55 minutes. The cake will deflate slightly as it cools. Set the pan on a rack to cool for about 15 minutes. Then use the parchment paper to lift the cake out of the pan and set it on the rack to cool completely.

6. Dust the top with confectioners' sugar just before serving, if desired. (Store the cake, well wrapped, at room temperature for up to two days. The apples on top will soften the cake as it sits.)

Use Another Pan

ROUND: Bake in a 9-inch round pan until puffed and golden, and a tester inserted into the center comes out clean, 45 to 55 minutes.

SHEET: Double the ingredients for the cake and bake in a 9 x 13-inch pan until puffed and golden, and a tester inserted into the center comes out clean, 50 to 60 minutes.

Flavor Variations

DOUBLE PEAR CAKE: Substitute thinly sliced pear for the apple and use pear sauce instead of applesauce. I like to add ½ teaspoon ground cardamom, too, but that's optional.

CARAMEL APPLE CAKE: Skip the apples on top and glaze the cake with Fudgy Caramel Icing (page 109) or soak it with Whiskey Caramel (page 126).

Dress It Up

Scoops of vanilla or caramel ice cream are just the thing to turn this stunning cake from snack to dessert.

warm
+ toasty
cakes

the recipes in this chapter highlight spicy, nutty, and herby flavors that make you want to curl up in an armchair with a slice of cake and a warm bev. I like to think of them as the coziest cakes, full of flavors that warm you from the inside out, like cinnamon and allspice, lots of toasted nuts, and sweet floral honey. If you don't regularly stock these ingredients in your pantry, hit the bulk bins at your local natural foods store and grab what you need for a cake or two. Then put on your softest pajamas, slip on some comfy slippers, and make yourself a warm and toasty cake.

Use Another Pan

LOAF: Bake in a 9 x 5 x 3-inch loaf pan until puffed and golden, and a skewer inserted into the center comes out clean, 55 to 65 minutes.

ROUND: Bake in a 9-inch round pan until puffed and golden, and a tester inserted into the center comes out clean, 35 to 45 minutes.

Flavor Variations

PEANUT BUTTER BANANA CAKE: Substitute an equal amount of natural peanut butter for the almond butter. Add Cocoa Glaze (page 135) if you are feeling indulgent.

STRAWBERRY BANANA-ALMOND BUTTER CAKE: Top the cake with Freeze-Dried Strawberry Glaze (page 75).

Dress It Up

Top slices of cake with Vanilla Bean Whip (page 182) or vanilla ice cream and fresh berries or shaved chocolate.

Almond Butter Banana Cake

My brother's family has dubbed this cake "better than banana bread," and chances are you might have all the ingredients in your pantry to make it right now. It hits the sweet spot between something wholesome and something indulgent, making it the perfect after-school or afternoon snack. Use natural almond butter here—the kind where you have to stir in the oil on top. I prefer a toasted variety for flavor, but untoasted works, too. You can also use peanut butter!

½ cup (100g) sugar

1 large egg

1½ cups (345g) mashed very ripe banana (about 3 bananas)

½ cup (120ml) whole milk

½ cup (120g) natural almond butter, well stirred

¼ cup (60ml) neutral oil, like canola or grapeseed

1 teaspoon vanilla extract

¾ teaspoon kosher salt

1¼ cups (160g) all-purpose flour

1½ teaspoons baking powder

½ teaspoon baking soda

1. Position a rack in the center of your oven and preheat the oven to 350°F. Butter or coat an 8-inch square baking pan with nonstick spray. Line the pan with a strip of parchment paper that hangs over two of the edges.

2. In a large bowl, whisk the sugar and egg until pale and foamy, about 1 minute. Add the banana, milk, almond butter, oil, vanilla, and salt. Whisk until smooth and emulsified.

3. Add the flour, baking powder, and baking soda and whisk until well-combined and completely smooth.

4. Pour the batter into the prepared pan, tap the pan gently on the counter to release any air bubbles, and smooth the top of the batter with an offset spatula.

5. Bake the cake until puffed and golden, and a tester inserted into the center comes out clean, 35 to 45 minutes. Set the pan on a rack to cool for about 15 minutes. Then use the parchment paper to lift the cake out of the pan and set it on the rack to cool completely. Enjoy warm or at room temperature. (Store the cake, well wrapped, in the fridge or at room temperature for up to three days.)

All the Spices Cake
with Vanilla Bean Glaze

Everyone needs a good back-pocket spice cake for the fall and winter, and this one fits the bill. I've added some tangy buttermilk to the mix to ensure this cake is soft, fluffy, and super flavorful. This spice mix is a great starting place, but feel free to modify it to suit your tastes. It's also a great canvas for chocolate or caramel toppings.

All the Spices Cake

¾ cup (150g) dark brown sugar

2 large eggs

1 cup (240ml) buttermilk, well shaken

½ cup (120ml) neutral oil, like canola or grapeseed

2 teaspoons ground cinnamon

1 teaspoon ground ginger

1 teaspoon vanilla bean paste or vanilla extract

½ teaspoon ground cardamom

¼ teaspoon ground cloves

¼ teaspoon freshly grated nutmeg

½ teaspoon kosher salt

1¼ cups (160g) all-purpose flour

1½ teaspoons baking powder

Vanilla Bean Glaze

1 cup (100g) confectioners' sugar

2 tablespoons milk, or more as needed

1 teaspoon vanilla bean paste or vanilla extract

Pinch of salt

1. Position a rack in the center of your oven and preheat the oven to 350°F. Butter or coat an 8-inch square baking pan with nonstick spray and line with a strip of parchment paper that hangs over two of the edges.

2. **MAKE THE CAKE:** In a large bowl, whisk the brown sugar and eggs until pale and foamy, about 1 minute. Add the buttermilk, oil, cinnamon, ginger, vanilla, cardamom, cloves, nutmeg, and salt and whisk until smooth and emulsified.

3. Add the flour and baking powder and whisk until well-combined and smooth.

4. Pour the batter into the prepared pan, tap the pan gently on the counter to remove any air bubbles, and smooth the top of the batter with an offset spatula.

5. Bake the cake until puffed and golden, and a tester inserted into the center comes out clean, 30 to 40 minutes. Set the pan on a rack to cool for about 15 minutes and then use the parchment paper to lift the cake out of the pan and set it on the rack to cool completely.

6. **MAKE THE GLAZE:** Combine the confectioners' sugar, 1 tablespoon of the milk, the vanilla, and salt together in a bowl and whisk until smooth. Add more milk, 1 teaspoon at a time, to make a thick but pourable glaze.

7. Pour the glaze over the cooled cake and let it set for 20 minutes before slicing the cake. (Store the cake, covered, at room temperature or in the fridge for up to three days.)

Use Another Pan

LOAF: Bake in a 9 x 5 x 3-inch loaf pan until puffed and golden, and a skewer inserted into the center comes out clean, 45 to 55 minutes. You'll need a half batch of glaze to coat the cake in a thin layer.

ROUND: Bake in a 9-inch round pan until puffed and golden, and a tester inserted into the center comes out clean, 30 to 40 minutes.

SHEET: Double the ingredients for the cake and bake in a 9 x 13-inch pan until puffed and golden, and a tester inserted into the center comes out clean, 35 to 45 minutes. Double the ingredients for the glaze, too.

Flavor Variations

CHAI MASALA SPICE CAKE: Replace the spice mix with 1½ teaspoons ground ginger, 1½ teaspoons ground cardamom, 1 teaspoon ground cinnamon, and ¼ teaspoon finely ground black pepper.

APPLE OR PEAR SPICE CAKE: Fold in 1 peeled and chopped apple or pear after you've stirred in the flour.

Dress It Up

Top the cake with Maple Coffee Glaze (page 91) or Fudgy Caramel Icing (page 109) and serve with Brown Sugar Whip (page 180)

Buttered Walnut Cake
with Maple Coffee Glaze

The extra step of cooking walnuts in butter may seem a little futzy to you, but it does double duty by toasting the nuts and browning the butter to add a more nutty flavor. This cake is delicious with a bit of this rich maple coffee glaze, but if you are a chocolate fan, a drizzle of Cocoa Glaze (page 135) wouldn't be out of place, either.

Buttered Walnut Cake

½ cup (113g) unsalted butter

1 cup (110g) finely chopped walnuts

¾ cup (150g) granulated sugar

2 large eggs

¾ cup (165g) sour cream

2 teaspoons vanilla extract

¾ teaspoon kosher salt

½ teaspoon instant espresso powder (optional)

1¼ cups (160g) all-purpose flour

1½ teaspoons baking powder

¼ teaspoon baking soda

Maple Coffee Glaze

1 cup (100g) confectioners' sugar

2 tablespoons maple syrup

1 to 2 tablespoons milk

½ teaspoon instant espresso powder

Pinch of salt

1. Position a rack in the center of your oven and preheat the oven to 350°F. Butter or coat an 8-inch square baking pan with nonstick spray. Line the pan with a strip of parchment paper that hangs over two of the edges.

2. **MAKE THE CAKE:** Add the butter to a medium saucepan or skillet and melt it over medium heat. Add the walnuts and toast the nuts in the butter, stirring constantly, for about 3 minutes. The butter will foam quite a bit, so make sure to keep stirring. When the nuts and butter are toasty and brown, pour the whole lot into a big bowl and let it cool for a few minutes.

3. Add the granulated sugar, eggs, sour cream, vanilla, salt, and espresso powder (if using) to the bowl with the walnuts and butter. Whisk until well-combined and emulsified.

4. Add the flour, baking powder, and baking soda and whisk until well-combined and smooth.

5. Pour the batter into the prepared pan, tap the pan gently on the counter to release any air bubbles, and smooth the top of the batter with an offset spatula.

recipe continues ⟶

6. Bake the cake until puffed and golden, and a tester inserted into the center comes out clean, 25 to 35 minutes. Set the pan on a rack to cool for about 15 minutes. Then use the parchment paper to lift the cake out of the pan and set it on the rack to cool completely.

7. **MAKE THE GLAZE:** Add the confectioners' sugar, maple syrup, 1 tablespoon of the milk, the espresso powder, and salt to a bowl. Whisk until smooth, adding a bit more milk, if necessary, to make a very thick but pourable glaze.

8. Pour the glaze over the cooled cake and let it set for about 20 minutes before slicing the cake. (Store the cake, covered, at room temperature for up to three days. The glaze will soften over time.)

Use Another Pan

BUNDT: Double the ingredients for the cake and bake in a prepared 15-cup Bundt pan until puffed and golden, and a skewer inserted into the center comes out clean, 55 to 65 minutes. Let the cake cool in the pan for 10 minutes, then invert it onto a rack to cool completely. Double the ingredients for the glaze, too.

LOAF: Bake in a 9 x 5 x 3-inch pan until puffed and golden, and a skewer inserted into the center comes out clean, 50 to 60 minutes. You'll need a half batch of glaze to coat the cake in a thin layer.

ROUND: Bake in a 9-inch round pan until puffed and golden, and a tester inserted into the center comes out clean, 25 to 35 minutes.

Flavor Variations

Top the cake with Vanilla Bean Glaze (page 88) or Cocoa Glaze (page 135).

MOCHA WALNUT-CARDAMOM CAKE: Add an additional ½ teaspoon instant espresso powder and 1 teaspoon ground cardamom to the walnut and butter mixture, and fold ½ cup (85g) chocolate chips or chopped chocolate into the batter. Top the cake with Cocoa Glaze (page 135).

Dress It Up

Top slices of cake with Coffee Whip (page 180) and shaved chocolate.

Powdered Donut Cake

Heavy on the butter and nutmeg, this cake has all the flavors of your favorite cake donut in a convenient square shape—no frying necessary! Just take my word for it, and don't wear a black shirt when you eat it. You are definitely going to get confectioners' sugar all over yourself with every bite.

Donut Cake

¾ cup (150g) granulated sugar

2 large eggs

1 cup (220g) sour cream

½ cup (113g) unsalted butter, melted

1¼ teaspoons freshly grated nutmeg

1 teaspoon vanilla extract

¾ teaspoon kosher salt

1½ cups (190g) all-purpose flour

1½ teaspoons baking powder

¼ teaspoon baking soda

Topping

1 tablespoon unsalted butter, melted

3 tablespoons confectioners' sugar

1. Position a rack in the center of your oven and preheat the oven to 350°F. Butter or coat an 8-inch square baking pan with nonstick spray. Line the pan with a strip of parchment paper that hangs over two of the edges.

2. MAKE THE CAKE: In a large bowl, whisk the granulated sugar and eggs until pale and foamy, about 1 minute. Add the sour cream, butter, nutmeg, vanilla, and salt. Whisk until smooth and emulsified.

3. Add the flour, baking powder, and baking soda. Whisk until well-combined and smooth.

4. Pour the batter into the pan and bake the cake until puffed and golden, and a skewer inserted into the center comes out clean, 25 to 35 minutes. Set the pan on a rack to cool for about 15 minutes. Then use the parchment paper to lift the cake out of the pan and set it on the rack to cool almost completely.

5. FINISH THE CAKE: While the cake is just warm to the touch, brush the top with the melted butter and dust with the confectioners' sugar. You should have a nice thick layer of confectioners' sugar—more than you think might be necessary. (Store the cake, covered, at room temperature for up to three days. The cake will absorb the sugar on top, so it might need a fresh dusting of confectioners' sugar after the second day.)

recipe continues ⟶

Use Another Pan

BUNDT: Double the recipe for the cake and bake in a prepared 15-cup Bundt pan until puffed and golden, and a skewer inserted into the center comes out clean, 50 to 60 minutes. Let the cake cool in the pan for 10 minutes, then invert it onto a rack to cool completely. Brush the warm cake with 4 tablespoons (65g) melted butter and dust with a generous amount of confectioners' sugar.

LOAF: Bake in a 9 x 5 x 3-inch loaf pan until puffed and golden, and a skewer inserted into the center comes out clean, 40 to 50 minutes.

ROUND: Bake in a 9-inch round pan until puffed and golden, and a tester inserted into the center comes out clean, 25 to 35 minutes.

Flavor Variations

BROWNED BUTTER DONUT CAKE: Brown the ½ cup (113g) butter using the instructions on page 24 and then proceed with the recipe as written.

CINNAMON SUGAR DONUT CAKE: Brush the cake with the melted butter, then sprinkle a combination of 2 tablespoons granulated sugar and 2 teaspoons ground cinnamon over the top instead of the confectioners' sugar.

GLAZED DONUT CAKE: Glaze the cake with Cocoa Glaze (page 135), Maple Coffee Glaze (page 91), or Vanilla Bean Glaze (page 88) instead of the butter and confectioners' sugar.

Dress It Up

Top slices of cake with ice cream and sliced fresh strawberries that have been tossed with a bit of granulated sugar.

Use Another Pan

CUPCAKES: Bake in a cupcake tin lined with paper liners, filling them no more than halfway full, until puffed and golden, and a tester inserted into the center comes out clean, 12 to 18 minutes. Makes 12 to 18 cupcakes.

ROUND: Bake in a 9-inch round pan until puffed and golden, and a tester inserted into the center comes out clean, 30 to 40 minutes.

SKILLET: Bake in a generously buttered 9-inch oven-safe skillet until puffed and golden, and a tester inserted into the center comes out clean, 30 to 40 minutes.

Flavor Variations

CARROT, RAISIN, AND WALNUT CAKE: Substitute orange zest for lemon, an equal amount of raisins for the dates, and walnuts for the pecans. Glaze the cake with Maple Coffee Glaze (page 91).

Dress It Up

Top slices of cake with dollops of Crème Fraîche Whip (page 180) or Honey Whip (page 181).

My Best Carrot Cake

Okay, okay, raisin haters—you win. But I will not give up fruit and nuts in my carrot cake. This one is packed with sticky-sweet chopped dates and toasty pecans. Both are totally optional, but I highly recommend them. And if you, like me, enjoy golden raisins in your carrot cake, feel free to toss in a handful instead of the dates. If you don't stock whole wheat flour in your pantry, you can substitute an equal amount of all-purpose flour or another whole-grain flour.

1 lemon

½ cup (100g) sugar

2 large eggs

¾ cup (180ml) neutral oil, like canola or grapeseed

1 teaspoon ground cardamom

½ teaspoon ground cinnamon

¼ teaspoon freshly grated nutmeg

¾ teaspoon kosher salt

¾ cup (95g) all-purpose flour

½ cup (65g) whole wheat flour

1½ teaspoons baking powder

½ teaspoon baking soda

2 cups (225g) peeled and grated carrots

½ cup (60g) chopped pitted dates

¾ cup (75g) chopped toasted pecans

Flaky salt, to finish (optional)

1. Position a rack in the center of your oven and preheat the oven to 350°F. Butter or coat an 8-inch square baking pan with nonstick spray. Line the pan with a strip of parchment paper that hangs over two of the edges.

2. Zest the lemon directly into a large bowl and add the sugar and eggs. Whisk the mixture until pale and foamy, about 1 minute. Add the oil, cardamom, cinnamon, nutmeg, and kosher salt. Whisk until smooth and emulsified.

3. Add the all-purpose flour, whole wheat flour, baking powder, and baking soda and whisk until well-combined and smooth. Then use a rubber spatula to fold in the grated carrots, dates, and ½ cup (50g) of the pecans.

4. Pour the batter into the prepared pan, tap the pan gently on the counter to release any air bubbles, and smooth the top of the batter with an offset spatula. Sprinkle the remaining ¼ cup (25g) pecans and a few flakes of flaky salt, if desired, over the top of the cake.

5. Bake the cake until puffed and golden, and a tester inserted into the center comes out clean, 30 to 40 minutes. Set the pan on a rack to cool for about 15 minutes. Then use the parchment paper to lift the cake out of the pan and set it on the rack to cool completely. (Store the cake, well wrapped, at room temperature for up to three days.)

Citrusy Almond Cornmeal Cake (Gluten-Free)

This gluten-free cake is dense, moist, and super citrusy. The pan is lined with almonds and sugar, making a perfectly crisp topping. Don't skip the syrup—it is sweet, tart, and packed with lots more citrus zest to make this cake a puckery treat. The syrup also extends the shelf life of the cake a bit, although I'm sure you won't have a problem polishing this off in a couple of days. You'll need two lemons and two tangerines for the cake and syrup.

Citrusy Almond Cornmeal Cake

1 cup (90g) sliced almonds

¾ cup (150g) plus 2 tablespoons sugar

1 lemon

1 tangerine or small orange

3 large eggs

½ cup (113g) unsalted butter, melted

¾ teaspoon kosher salt

1½ cups (165g) almond flour

½ cup (65g) finely ground yellow cornmeal

1 tablespoon cornstarch

2 teaspoons baking powder

Citrus Syrup

¼ cup (50g) sugar

2 teaspoons finely grated lemon zest

2 teaspoons finely grated tangerine or orange zest

2 tablespoons lemon juice

2 tablespoons tangerine or orange juice

1. Position a rack in the center of your oven and preheat the oven to 350°F. Very generously butter an 8-inch square baking pan, line it with a square of parchment paper, and then butter the paper.

2. **MAKE THE CAKE:** Arrange the almonds over the parchment paper in an even layer (there will be some overlap) and then sprinkle 2 tablespoons of the sugar over the almonds.

3. Zest the lemon and tangerine (or orange) into a large bowl and add the eggs and the remaining ¾ cup (150g) sugar. Whisk until pale and foamy, about 1 minute. Add the butter and salt and whisk until smooth and emulsified.

4. Add the almond flour, cornmeal, cornstarch, and baking powder. Whisk until well-combined and smooth.

5. Gently pour the batter over the almonds in the pan, tap the pan gently on the counter to release any air bubbles, and smooth the top of the batter with an offset spatula.

6. Bake the cake until puffed and golden, and a tester inserted into the center comes out clean, 35 to 45 minutes. Set the cake on a rack to cool for 15 minutes.

7.   **MAKE THE SYRUP:** Combine the sugar, lemon zest, tangerine zest, lemon juice, and tangerine juice in a small saucepan over medium-high heat. Stir occasionally until the sugar dissolves. Remove from the heat.

8.   After the cake has cooled for 15 minutes, carefully invert it onto a serving plate, remove the parchment, and spoon the syrup over the top. Let the syrup soak into the cake for 1 hour, then serve the cake warm or at room temperature. (Store the cake, well wrapped, at room temperature for up to three days.)

Use Another Pan

ROUND: Bake in a 9-inch round pan until puffed and golden, and a tester inserted into the center comes out clean, 35 to 45 minutes.

Dress It Up

Serve slices of cake with Crème Fraîche Whip (page 180) or Honey Whip (page 181).

Use Another Pan

LOAF: Bake in a 9 x 5 x 3-inch loaf pan until puffed and golden, and a skewer inserted into the center comes out clean, 45 to 55 minutes.

ROUND: Bake in a 9-inch round pan until puffed and golden, and a tester inserted into the center comes out clean, 30 to 40 minutes.

SKILLET: Bake in a generously buttered 9-inch oven-safe skillet until puffed and golden, and a tester inserted into the center comes out clean, 30 to 40 minutes.

Flavor Variations

BLUEBERRY OR RASPBERRY CORNMEAL CAKE: Fold in 1 cup (160g) of fresh blueberries or raspberries. Top with Lemon Glaze (page 44) or Fresh Raspberry Glaze (page 57).

MEYER LEMON–HONEY CORNMEAL CAKE: Whisk the zest of 1 Meyer lemon along with the sugar, honey, and eggs. Top the cooled cake with Lemon Glaze (page 44) made with a Meyer lemon.

Corn Cake with Honey

Cornmeal cake has always been one of my favorites because it has a sweet and savory vibe that makes it equally welcome at the breakfast, dinner, and dessert tables. I have it on my one-year-old neighbor Jack's authority that this one is very tasty as is, but there are lots of ways to dress it up; I've listed a few here to get you started. Make it extra corny by folding in ½ cup (50g) of the sweetest corn kernels you can find.

½ cup (100g) plus 2 teaspoons sugar

¼ cup (60ml) runny honey

2 large eggs

1 cup (220g) sour cream

½ cup (113g) unsalted butter, melted

¾ teaspoon kosher salt

1 cup (128g) all-purpose flour

½ cup (65g) finely ground cornmeal

1½ teaspoons baking powder

½ teaspoon baking soda

Flaky salt, to finish (optional)

Dress It Up

Top slices of cake with Crème Fraîche Whip (page 180) and fresh fruit.

1. Position a rack in the center of your oven and preheat the oven to 350°F. Butter or coat an 8-inch square baking pan with nonstick spray. Line the pan with a strip of parchment paper that hangs over two of the edges.

2. In a large bowl, whisk ½ cup (100g) of the sugar, the honey, and eggs until pale and foamy, about 1 minute. Add the sour cream, butter, and kosher salt. Whisk until smooth and emulsified.

3. Add the flour, cornmeal, baking powder, and baking soda. Whisk until well-combined and smooth.

4. Pour the batter into the prepared pan, tap the pan gently on the counter to release any air bubbles, and smooth the top of the batter with an offset spatula. Sprinkle with the remaining 2 teaspoons sugar and add a sprinkle of flaky salt, if desired.

5. Bake the cake until puffed and golden, and a tester inserted into the center comes out clean, 30 to 40 minutes. Set the pan on a rack to cool for about 15 minutes. Then use the parchment paper to lift the cake out of the pan and set it on the rack to cool completely. (Store the cake, well wrapped, at room temperature for up to three days.)

Spiced Honey Cake

I usually pick a floral or citrusy honey for this cake, like wildflower or clover rather than a dark, strongly flavored variety, but you can use any honey you prefer. Don't skip the sliced almonds on top—they add a lovely crunch and texture.

¾ cup (215g) runny honey

¼ cup (50g) light brown sugar

1 large egg

½ cup (120ml) neutral oil, like canola or grapeseed

½ cup (120ml) buttermilk, well shaken

1 teaspoon vanilla extract

½ teaspoon ground cinnamon

¾ teaspoon kosher salt

1¼ cups (160g) all-purpose flour

1½ teaspoons baking powder

¼ teaspoon baking soda

½ cup (45g) sliced almonds (optional)

1. Position a rack in the center of your oven and preheat the oven to 350°F. Butter or coat an 8-inch square baking pan with nonstick spray. Line the pan with a strip of parchment paper that hangs over two of the edges.

2. In a large bowl, whisk the honey, brown sugar, egg, oil, buttermilk, vanilla, cinnamon, and salt until smooth and emulsified.

3. Add the flour, baking powder, and baking soda and whisk until well-combined and smooth.

4. Pour the batter into the prepared pan, tap the pan gently on the counter to release any air bubbles, and smooth the top of the batter with an offset spatula. Scatter the almonds over the top, if desired.

5. Bake the cake until puffed and golden, and a tester inserted into the center comes out clean, 25 to 35 minutes. Set the pan on a rack to cool for about 15 minutes. Then use the parchment paper to lift the cake out of the pan and set it on the rack to cool completely. Serve warm or at room temperature. (Store the cake, well wrapped, at room temperature for up to three days.)

Use Another Pan

BUNDT: Double the ingredients for the cake (skip the sliced almond sprinkle) and bake in a prepared 15-cup Bundt pan until puffed and golden, and a skewer inserted into the center comes out clean, 40 to 50 minutes. Let the cake cool in the pan for 10 minutes, then invert onto a rack to cool completely.

LOAF: Use ¼ cup (22g) sliced almonds instead of ½ cup (45g) for the topping. Bake in a 9 x 5 x 3-inch loaf pan until puffed and golden, and a skewer inserted into the center comes out clean, 35 to 45 minutes.

ROUND: Bake in a 9-inch round pan until puffed and golden, and a tester inserted into the center comes out clean, 30 to 40 minutes.

Flavor Variations

APPLE OR PEAR HONEY CAKE: Fold in 1 chopped peeled apple after you add the flour and leavening. This variation may take a few more minutes to bake.

BLACKBERRY HONEY CAKE: Sprinkle 1 cup (170g) fresh blackberries over the top of the batter before adding the almonds. This variation may take a few more minutes to bake.

Dress It Up

Top slices of cake with Orange Blossom Whip (page 181) and fresh berries.

Use Another Pan

BUNDT: Double the ingredients for the cake, skip the sugar and flaky salt sprinkle, and bake in a prepared 15-cup Bundt pan until puffed and golden, and a skewer inserted into the center comes out clean, 40 to 50 minutes. Let the cake cool in the pan for 10 minutes, then invert it onto a rack to cool completely.

LOAF: Bake in a 9 x 5 x 3-inch loaf pan until puffed and golden, and a skewer inserted into the center comes out clean, 35 to 45 minutes.

ROUND: Bake in a 9-inch round pan until puffed and golden, and a tester inserted into the center comes out clean, 35 to 45 minutes.

Flavor Variations

SUPER-CITRUS, CURRANT, AND ROSEMARY CAKE: Zest additional lemon into the batter. Skip the sugar and flaky salt sprinkle, then top the cooled cake with Lemon Glaze (page 44).

Dress It Up

Serve slices of cake with lemon ice cream or sorbet or Whipped Vanilla Mascarpone (page 182).

Lemony Currant and Rosemary Cake

I am lucky to live just around the corner from Ovenly, one of the best bakeries in New York City. When Agatha Kulaga and Erin Patinkin opened Ovenly in 2010, the first scone on their menu had this unexpected combination of sweet dried currants and savory rosemary. I have borrowed that surprising and delicious pairing for this buttery cake that is lightened with a bit of lemon zest. Meyer lemon is especially tasty with the currants and rosemary.

1 lemon

¾ cup (150g) plus 2 teaspoons sugar

2 large eggs

½ cup (110g) sour cream

½ cup (113g) unsalted butter, melted

4 teaspoons very finely chopped fresh rosemary

1 teaspoon vanilla bean paste or vanilla extract

¾ teaspoon kosher salt

1½ cups (190g) all-purpose flour

¾ cup (110g) dried currants

1½ teaspoons baking powder

¼ teaspoon baking soda

Flaky salt, to finish (optional)

1. Position a rack in the center of your oven and preheat the oven to 350°F. Butter or coat an 8-inch square baking pan with nonstick spray. Line the pan with a strip of parchment paper that hangs over two of the edges.

2. Zest the lemon directly into a large bowl. Add ¾ cup (150g) of the sugar and the eggs and whisk until pale and foamy, about 1 minute. Add the sour cream, butter, rosemary, vanilla, and kosher salt. Whisk until smooth.

3. Add the flour, currants, baking powder, and baking soda to the bowl and stir with a rubber spatula until well-combined and smooth.

4. Pour the batter into the prepared pan, tap the pan gently on the counter to release any air bubbles, and smooth the top of the batter with an offset spatula. Sprinkle the remaining 2 teaspoons sugar and the flaky salt (if using) over the top.

5. Bake the cake until puffed and golden, and a tester inserted into the center comes out clean, 35 to 45 minutes. Set the pan on a rack to cool for about 15 minutes. Then use the parchment paper to lift the cake out of the pan and set it on the rack to cool completely. (Store the cake, well wrapped, at room temperature for up to three days.)

Morning Glory Cake

I can never resist morning glory muffins when I see them in a
bakery case. Every place makes them a little differently, and
they can include any combination of pineapple, carrot, banana,
apple, pear, nuts, seeds, and coconut. I've tried to streamline the
ingredients in this version, while holding true to the empty-your-
pantry nature of a morning glory. Grate the apple and carrot
on the large holes of a box grater; no need to peel first. I usually
add a pinch of fennel seed, too, but it's a strong flavor, so I didn't
include it here. If you're a fennel fan, feel free to add a bit!

1 lemon

¾ cup (150g) sugar

2 large eggs

¾ cup (180ml) neutral oil, such as
canola or grapeseed

½ teaspoon ground cardamom

½ teaspoon ground cinnamon

¾ teaspoon kosher salt

1 cup (100g) grated apple (1 medium
apple)

1 cup (70g) grated carrot (1 large
carrot)

½ cup (80g) very well-drained canned
crushed pineapple or finely chopped
fresh pineapple

½ cup (50g) chopped toasted pecans

1¼ cups (160g) all-purpose flour

1½ teaspoons baking powder

½ teaspoon baking soda

1 tablespoon flax seeds (optional)

1. Position a rack in the center of your oven and preheat the
oven to 350°F. Butter or coat an 8-inch square baking pan with
nonstick spray. Line the pan with a strip of parchment paper
that hangs over two of the edges.

2. Zest the lemon into a large bowl. Add the sugar and eggs
and whisk the mixture until pale and foamy, about 1 minute.
Add the oil, cardamom, cinnamon, and salt. Whisk until smooth
and emulsified.

3. Switch to a rubber spatula and stir in the grated apple,
grated carrot, pineapple, and ¼ cup (25g) of the pecans.

4. Add the flour, baking powder, and baking soda and stir until
well-combined.

5. Pour the batter into the prepared pan, tap the pan gently
on the counter to release any air bubbles, and smooth the
top of the batter with an offset spatula. Sprinkle the remaining
¼ cup (25g) pecans and the flax seeds (if using) over the top
of the cake.

6. Bake the cake until puffed and golden, and a tester inserted into the center comes out clean, 45 to 55 minutes. Set the pan on a rack to cool for about 15 minutes. Then use the parchment paper to lift the cake out of the pan and set it on the rack to cool completely. (Store the cake, well wrapped, at room temperature for two days or in the fridge for three days.)

Use Another Pan

LOAF: Bake in a 9 x 5 x 3-inch loaf pan until puffed and golden, and a skewer inserted into the center comes out clean, 50 to 60 minutes.

ROUND: Bake in a 9-inch round pan until puffed and golden, and a tester inserted into the center comes out clean, 45 to 55 minutes.

Flavor Variations

APPLE-CARROT-COCONUT MORNING GLORY CAKE: Omit the pineapple and increase the grated carrot and grated apple to 1¼ cups (125g) each. Add ½ cup (40g) unsweetened shredded coconut along with the flour. Sprinkle an additional tablespoon of coconut on top of the cake along with the nuts and flax seeds (if using).

Salty Caramel Peanut Butter Cake

Make sure to use a commercial peanut butter like Skippy here, as natural peanut butter will make this cake extra oily. This style of icing is pretty old school, and you'll find similar recipes in vintage cookbooks listed as penuche. Its fudgy rich texture is the perfect match for this sweet-salty cake. Don't be shy with the flaky salt sprinkle at the end.

Peanut Butter Cake

¾ cup (150g) light brown sugar

2 large eggs

½ cup (125g) smooth peanut butter

½ cup (120ml) buttermilk, well shaken

½ cup (120ml) neutral oil, like canola or grapeseed

1 teaspoon vanilla extract

½ teaspoon kosher salt

1¼ cups (160g) all-purpose flour

1½ teaspoons baking powder

¼ teaspoon baking soda

Fudgy Caramel Icing

¼ cup (55g) unsalted butter

½ cup (100g) light brown sugar

¼ cup (60ml) heavy cream

1 tablespoon water

Pinch of kosher salt

½ cup (50g) confectioners' sugar

Flaky salt, to finish (optional)

1. Position a rack in the center of your oven and preheat the oven to 350°F. Butter or coat an 8-inch square baking pan with nonstick spray. Line the pan with a strip of parchment paper that hangs over two of the edges.

2. **MAKE THE CAKE:** In a large bowl, whisk the brown sugar and eggs until pale and foamy, about 1 minute. Add the peanut butter and whisk until smooth. Add the buttermilk, oil, vanilla, and kosher salt. Whisk until smooth and emulsified.

3. Add the flour, baking powder, and baking soda and whisk until well-combined and smooth.

4. Pour the batter into the prepared pan, tap the pan gently on the counter to release any air bubbles, and smooth the top of the batter with an offset spatula.

5. Bake the cake until puffed and golden, and a tester inserted into the center comes out clean, 35 to 45 minutes. Set the pan on a rack to cool for about 15 minutes. Then use the parchment paper to lift the cake out of the pan and set it on the rack to cool completely.

recipe continues ⟶

6. **MAKE THE ICING:** Melt the butter, brown sugar, cream, and water together in a saucepan set over medium heat. Bring the mixture to a full rolling boil and cook for 3 more minutes. Turn off the heat and let the mixture cool for 3 minutes, stirring once or twice to release the heat. After 3 minutes, whisk in the kosher salt and confectioners' sugar until smooth. Immediately spread the icing over the cooled cake and sprinkle with flaky salt, if using. Let the icing set for about 20 minutes before slicing the cake. (Store the cake, covered, at room temperature for up to three days. This cake is also delicious cold from the fridge.)

Use Another Pan

LOAF: Bake in a 9 x 5 x 3-inch loaf pan until puffed and golden, and a skewer inserted into the center comes out clean, 50 to 60 minutes. You'll need a half batch of icing to coat the cake in a thin layer.

ROUND: Bake in a 9-inch round pan until puffed and golden, and a tester inserted into the center comes out clean, 35 to 45 minutes.

Dress It Up

Top slices of cake with scoops of ice cream (chocolate or vanilla would be my picks) and Cocoa Whip (page 180). If you're feeling it, add sliced fresh strawberries or raspberries, too!

Flavor Variations

COOKIE BUTTER CAKE: Substitute an equal amount of speculoos cookie butter for the peanut butter, and add ½ teaspoon ground cinnamon with the vanilla and kosher salt. Top with the Fudgy Caramel Icing (page 109), or Maple Coffee Glaze (page 91), if desired.

PEANUT BUTTER CHOCOLATE CAKE: Fold ½ cup (85g) chopped chocolate or chocolate chips into the batter before you pour it into the pan. Top the finished cake with Fluffy Chocolate Frosting (page 165).

PEANUT BUTTER AND JAM CAKE: Dollop ¼ cup (60g) of your favorite jam in teaspoon-size blobs over the batter in the pan and then use a wooden skewer or toothpick to swirl the jam into the batter. This may take a few passes—don't be afraid to get in there and really swirl it around. Skip the icing and dust the cooled cake with confectioners' sugar instead.

Seedy Zucchini Cake

A mix of seeds adds lots of crunch to this light, slightly wholesome zucchini cake. I've provided my favorite mix here, but any combination of sliced almonds, millet, or flax, sesame, hemp, chia, or poppy seeds would be delicious additions. This is one of the recipes where the bulk bins at your supermarket are going to be your best friend.

2 tablespoons poppy seeds

2 tablespoons millet

2 tablespoons flax seeds

1 lemon

¾ cup (150g) sugar

2 large eggs

¾ cup (180ml) neutral oil, like canola or grapeseed

1 teaspoon ground cinnamon

¾ teaspoon kosher salt

2¼ cups (225g) grated zucchini (use large holes of a box grater), squeezed to remove excess moisture

1 cup (128g) all-purpose flour

½ cup (65g) whole wheat flour

1 teaspoon baking powder

½ teaspoon baking soda

1. Position a rack in the center of your oven and preheat the oven to 350°F. Butter or coat an 8-inch square baking pan with nonstick spray. Line the pan with a strip of parchment paper that hangs over two of the edges.

2. Stir the poppy seeds, millet, and flax seeds together in a small bowl. Zest the lemon directly into a large bowl. Add the sugar and eggs to the zest and whisk until pale and foamy, about 1 minute. Add the oil, cinnamon, and salt and whisk until smooth and emulsified. Use a rubber spatula to stir in the grated zucchini and 4 tablespoons of the seed mixture.

3. Add the all-purpose flour, whole wheat flour, baking powder, and baking soda and stir until well-combined and smooth, making sure to scrape the bottom and sides of the bowl.

4. Pour the batter into the prepared pan, tap the pan gently on the counter to release any air bubbles, and smooth the top of the batter with an offset spatula. Sprinkle the remaining seed mixture over the top of the cake.

5. Bake the cake until puffed and golden, and a tester inserted into the center comes out clean, 35 to 45 minutes. Set the cake on a rack to cool for about 15 minutes. Then use the parchment paper to lift the cake out of the pan to cool completely. (Store the cake, well wrapped, at room temperature for two days.)

Flavor Variations

LEMONY ZUCCHINI CAKE:
Top the cooled cake with
Lemon Glaze (page 44) and a
sprinkle of grated zest for an
extra hit of lemon flavor.

Use Another Pan

LOAF: Bake in a 9 x 5 x 3-inch
loaf pan until puffed and
golden, and a skewer inserted
into the center comes out
clean, 45 to 55 minutes.

ROUND: Bake in a 9-inch
round pan until puffed and
golden, and a tester inserted
into the center comes out
clean, 35 to 45 minutes.

Simple Sesame Cake

This cake gets a double dose of sesame, with tahini and sesame seeds in the batter and lots of crunchy sesame seeds to coat the pan, too. I like the confetti effect of a combination of black and white sesame seeds, but there's no need to go out and buy both if you don't already have them in your pantry. If you are just using one type, white sesame seeds are the way to go.

6 tablespoons (50g) sesame seeds

¾ cup (150g) plus 1 tablespoon sugar

1 large egg

½ cup (120ml) whole milk

½ cup (120ml) tahini, well stirred

¼ cup (60ml) neutral oil, like canola or grapeseed

1 teaspoon vanilla extract

¾ teaspoon kosher salt

1¼ cups (160g) all-purpose flour

1½ teaspoons baking powder

¼ teaspoon baking soda

1. Position a rack in the center of your oven and preheat the oven to 350°F. Generously butter or coat an 8-inch square baking pan with nonstick spray and line it with a square of parchment paper that overhangs the sides. Butter or coat the parchment paper with nonstick spray, then sprinkle 2 tablespoons of the sesame seeds on the bottom and about 1 inch up the sides of the pan. Some of the pan will still be exposed, and that's okay.

2. In a large bowl, whisk ¾ cup (150g) of the sugar and the egg until pale and foamy, about 1 minute. Add the milk, tahini, oil, vanilla, and salt. Whisk until smooth and emulsified.

3. Add the flour, 3 tablespoons of the sesame seeds, the baking powder, and baking soda. Whisk until well-combined and smooth.

4. Pour the batter into the prepared pan, tap the pan gently on the counter to release any air bubbles, and smooth the top of the batter with an offset spatula. Sprinkle the remaining tablespoon sugar and the remaining tablespoon sesame seeds on top of the cake.

recipe continues $\longrightarrow$

5. Bake the cake until puffed and golden, and a tester inserted into the center comes out clean, 25 to 35 minutes. Set the cake on a rack to cool for about 15 minutes. Then use the parchment paper to lift the cake out of the pan to cool completely. (Store the cake, well wrapped, at room temperature for up to three days.)

Flavor Variations

PEACH AND RASPBERRY SESAME CAKE: Slice 1 small pitted peach into ½-inch slices. Arrange the slices over the top of the batter in a single layer, scatter ½ cup (70g) fresh raspberries over the top, then sprinkle with the sugar and sesame seeds.

CHOCOLATE AND SESAME CAKE: Fold ½ cup (85g) chopped chocolate or chocolate chips into the batter just before it goes into the pan.

SUPER SESAME CAKE: Omit the sugar and sesame seeds on top of the cake and make a Tahini Glaze by whisking 1 cup (100g) of confectioners' sugar with ¼ cup (60ml) tahini, a pinch of salt, and 1 to 2 tablespoons hot water. Pour the glaze over the cooled cake.

Use Another Pan

LOAF: Bake in a 9 x 5 x 3-inch loaf pan until puffed and golden, and a skewer inserted into the center comes out clean, 40 to 50 minutes. Sprinkle 1 teaspoon of sugar (instead of 1 tablespoon) and 2 teaspoons of sesame seeds on top.

ROUND: Bake in a 9-inch round pan until puffed and golden, and a tester inserted into the center comes out clean, 25 to 35 minutes.

Dress It Up

Serve slices of cake with dollops of Brown Sugar Whip (page 180) or Whipped Vanilla Mascarpone (page 182) and fresh berries.

Use Another Pan

LOAF: Bake in a 9 x 5 x 3-inch loaf pan until puffed and golden, and a skewer inserted into the center comes out clean, 40 to 50 minutes.

ROUND: Bake in a 9-inch round pan until puffed and golden, and a tester inserted into the center comes out clean, 30 to 40 minutes.

Flavor Variations

OATMEAL RAISIN CAKE: Substitute raisins for the chocolate chips. You can also add a handful of walnuts or white chocolate chips for a little flair.

Dress It Up

Serve warm slices of cake with vanilla ice cream or dollops of Brown Sugar Whip (page 180).

Oatmeal Chocolate Chip Cake

This cake has all the flavors you love in an oatmeal cookie, but in a fluffy and sliceable form with lots of chocolate throughout. The oats give this cake a bit of a wholesome vibe, but not too wholesome, if you know what I mean. I love a combination of milk and semisweet chocolate here, but you can use whatever you like. White chocolate or caramelized white chocolate, like Valrhona Dulcey, would be great, too.

1 cup (200g) light or dark brown sugar

2 large eggs

1 cup (240ml) whole milk

¼ cup (60ml) neutral oil, like canola or grapeseed

¼ cup (55g) unsalted butter, melted

1 teaspoon ground cinnamon

1 teaspoon vanilla extract

¾ teaspoon kosher salt

A few grates of nutmeg

1¼ cups (160g) all-purpose flour

¾ cup (120g) chocolate chips (any variety)

½ cup (45g) plus 2 tablespoons old-fashioned rolled oats

1½ teaspoons baking powder

¼ teaspoon baking soda

1. Position a rack in the center of your oven and preheat the oven to 350°F. Butter or coat an 8-inch square baking pan with nonstick spray. Line the pan with a strip of parchment paper that hangs over two of the edges.

2. In a large bowl, whisk the brown sugar and eggs until pale and foamy, about 1 minute. Add the milk, oil, butter, cinnamon, vanilla, salt, and nutmeg. Whisk until smooth and emulsified.

3. Add the flour, chocolate chips, ½ cup (45g) of the oats, the baking powder, and baking soda and stir with a rubber spatula until well-combined and smooth.

4. Pour the batter into the prepared pan, tap the pan gently on the counter to release any air bubbles, and smooth the top of the batter with an offset spatula. Sprinkle the remaining 2 tablespoons oats over the batter.

5. Bake the cake until puffed and golden, and a tester inserted into the center comes out clean, 30 to 40 minutes. There may be a bit of chocolate on the tester. Set the pan on a rack to cool for about 15 minutes. Then use the parchment paper to lift the cake out of the pan and set it on the rack to cool completely. (Store the cake, well wrapped, at room temperature for up to three days.)

Gingery Sweet Potato Cake

There is a sneaky pear in this cake that adds a bit of additional moisture and sweetness, but its flavor mostly melts into the background. Any sweet, slightly soft pear will do the trick. You can also try adding ½ cup (50g) of golden raisins. I love raisins, but for some reason lots of people don't, so proceed with caution.

⅓ cup (67g) granulated sugar

2 large eggs

¾ cup (180ml) neutral oil, like canola or grapeseed

2 teaspoons ground ginger

1 teaspoon ground cinnamon

¾ teaspoon kosher salt

2 cups (135g) grated peeled sweet potato (use large holes of a box grater)

½ cup (100g) grated peeled pear (use large holes of a box grater)

½ cup (50g) finely chopped crystallized ginger (optional)

1½ cups (190g) all-purpose flour

2 teaspoons baking powder

¼ teaspoon baking soda

1 tablespoon turbinado sugar (optional)

1. Position a rack in the center of your oven and preheat the oven to 350°F. Butter or coat an 8-inch square baking pan with nonstick spray. Line the pan with a strip of parchment paper that hangs over two of the edges.

2. In a large bowl, whisk the granulated sugar and eggs until pale and foamy, about 1 minute. Add the oil, ground ginger, cinnamon, and salt. Whisk until smooth and emulsified. Use a rubber spatula to stir in the sweet potato, pear, and ¼ cup (25g) of the crystallized ginger (if using).

3. Add the flour, baking powder, and baking soda and stir until well-combined and smooth, scraping down the bowl as you go.

4. Pour the batter into the prepared pan, tap the pan gently on the counter to release any air bubbles, and smooth the top of the batter with an offset spatula. Sprinkle with the remaining ¼ cup (25g) crystallized ginger and the turbinado sugar (if using).

5. Bake the cake until puffed and golden, and a tester inserted into the center comes out clean, 30 to 40 minutes. Set the pan on a rack to cool for about 15 minutes. Then use the parchment paper to lift the cake out of the pan and set it on the rack to cool completely. (Store the cake, well wrapped, at room temperature for up to three days.)

Use Another Pan

LOAF: Bake in a 9 x 5 x 3-inch loaf pan until puffed and golden, and a skewer inserted into the center comes out clean, 40 to 50 minutes.

ROUND: Bake in a 9-inch round pan until puffed and golden, and a tester inserted into the center comes out clean, 30 to 40 minutes.

Flavor Variations

GINGERY BUTTERNUT SQUASH CAKE: Substitute an equal amount of grated peeled butternut squash for the sweet potato and use a sweet apple instead of the pear.

Dress It Up

Top slices of cake with Vanilla Bean Whip (page 182) or Honey Whip (page 181) and fresh fruit, or serve with ice cream and a drizzle of Whiskey Caramel (page 126).

Sparkling Gingerbread

This spicy gingerbread gets three hits of ginger—crystallized, fresh, and ground—for lots of punchy flavor in an easy-to-stir batter. You can grate the fresh ginger with a Microplane; you don't even need to peel it. The cake's sparkling, crispy top comes from a generous sprinkle of turbinado sugar, but it's also delicious with a bit of citrus or a chocolate glaze instead.

½ cup (100g) dark brown sugar

2 large eggs

½ cup (120ml) buttermilk, well shaken

½ cup (113g) unsalted butter, melted

¼ cup (80g) unsulfured molasses (not blackstrap)

1 tablespoon finely grated fresh ginger

1 tablespoon ground ginger

1 teaspoon ground cinnamon

⅛ teaspoon ground cloves

¾ teaspoon kosher salt

1½ cups (190g) all-purpose flour

1½ teaspoons baking powder

½ teaspoon baking soda

¼ cup (25g) finely chopped crystallized ginger

2 tablespoons turbinado sugar

1. Position a rack in the center of your oven and preheat the oven to 350°F. Butter or coat an 8-inch square baking pan with nonstick spray. Line the pan with a strip of parchment paper that hangs over two of the edges, then butter or spray the paper, too.

2. In a large bowl, whisk the brown sugar and eggs until pale and foamy, about 1 minute. Add the buttermilk, butter, molasses, fresh and ground ginger, cinnamon, cloves, and salt. Whisk until smooth and emulsified.

3. Add the flour, baking powder, and baking soda and whisk until well-combined and smooth. Use a rubber spatula to fold in the crystallized ginger.

4. Pour the batter into the prepared pan, tap the pan gently on the counter to release any air bubbles, and smooth the top of the batter. Sprinkle the turbinado sugar evenly over the top.

5. Bake the cake until puffed and golden, and a skewer inserted into the center comes out clean, 30 to 40 minutes. Set the cake on a rack to cool for about 15 minutes. Then use the parchment paper to lift the cake out of the pan and set it on the rack to cool completely. (Store the cake, well wrapped, at room temperature for up to three days.)

recipe continues ⟶

Use Another Pan

BUNDT: Double the ingredients for the cake (skip the turbinado sugar sprinkle at the end) and bake in a prepared 15-cup Bundt pan until puffed and golden, and a skewer inserted into the center comes out clean, 50 to 60 minutes. Let the cake cool in the pan for 10 minutes, then invert it onto a rack to cool completely.

LOAF:. Pour the batter into a 9 x 5 x 3-inch loaf pan and sprinkle 1 tablespoon of turbinado sugar on top instead of 2. Bake until puffed and golden, and a skewer inserted into the center comes out clean, 50 to 60 minutes.

ROUND: Bake in a 9-inch round pan until puffed and golden, and a tester inserted into the center comes out clean, 30 to 40 minutes.

Flavor Variations

CRANBERRY GINGERBREAD: Before you sprinkle the turbinado sugar over the cake batter, scatter 1 cup (100g) fresh or frozen cranberries over the batter, then sprinkle the turbinado sugar on top of the cranberries.

GRAPEFRUIT GINGERBREAD: Omit the turbinado sugar on top of the cake batter. Bake as directed and then glaze the cooled cake with Grapefruit Glaze (page 50).

Dress It Up

Serve slices of cake with scoops of ice cream for a simple and satisfying dessert. Add Whiskey Caramel (page 126) to take it over the top.

Sticky Whiskey Date Cake

Dates can be kind of annoying to chop with a knife because they are very sticky, so I like to snip them into little pieces with kitchen scissors. Make sure to use fresh, soft Medjool dates in this cake, as other varieties won't work as well. You can drench the warm cake in caramel sauce and serve immediately, or keep the cake and sauce separate if you are serving later (just be sure to warm the caramel in a microwave or warm-water bath). This caramel is a nice addition to lots of other recipes, and as always, feel free to skip the whiskey.

Whiskey Date Cake

1 cup (150g) finely chopped pitted Medjool dates (about 10 dates)

½ teaspoon baking soda

½ cup (60ml) boiling water

⅓ cup (67g) dark brown sugar

2 large eggs

½ cup (120ml) whole milk

½ cup (113g) unsalted butter, melted

1 tablespoon whiskey

¾ teaspoon kosher salt

1 teaspoon instant espresso powder (optional)

1 teaspoon ground ginger

½ teaspoon ground cinnamon

¼ teaspoon ground cloves

1¼ cups (160g) all-purpose flour

1½ teaspoons baking powder

1. Position a rack in the center of your oven and preheat the oven to 350°F. Butter or coat an 8-inch square baking pan with nonstick spray. Line the pan with a strip of parchment paper that hangs over two of the edges.

2. **MAKE THE CAKE:** In a large bowl, combine the dates, baking soda, and boiling water. Let the mixture sit for 5 minutes, then use a fork to thoroughly mash the dates into a chunky paste. Add the brown sugar and eggs and whisk until well-combined. Add the milk, butter, whiskey, salt, espresso powder (if using), ginger, cinnamon, and cloves. Whisk until well-combined and emulsified.

3. Add the flour and baking powder. Whisk until well-combined and smooth.

4. Pour the batter into the prepared pan and tap the pan gently on the counter to remove any air bubbles.

5. Bake the cake until puffed and golden, and a tester inserted into the center comes out clean, 30 to 40 minutes. Set the pan on a rack to cool.

recipe and ingredients continue ⟶

Whiskey Caramel

⅓ cup (67g) dark brown sugar

2 tablespoons water

¼ cup (55g) unsalted butter

¼ cup (60ml) heavy cream

1 tablespoon whiskey

6. **MAKE THE CARAMEL:** Stir the brown sugar and water together in a small saucepan. Set the pan over medium heat and bring the mixture to a boil, swirling the pan occasionally. Cook the caramel, again swirling the pan occasionally, until it is a deep amber and you see the first wisps of smoke, about 5 minutes. Don't walk away from the pan during this process; you want the sugar to be deeply caramelized but not burnt. Turn off the heat and carefully add the butter and cream; the mixture will spit and sputter a bit. Add the whiskey and whisk until smooth. Cool the sauce slightly until thickened but still a bit warm.

7. Pour the caramel over the cake in the pan and serve the cake while the caramel is still warm. (Store the cake, covered, in the fridge for up to two days. Alternatively, store the cake and caramel separately. The caramel can be kept in a jar in the fridge for about a week, then warmed slightly before serving. Top slices of cake with warm caramel.)

Use Another Pan

ROUND: Bake in a 9-inch round pan until puffed and golden, and a tester inserted into the center comes out clean, 30 to 40 minutes.

Flavor Variations

CHOCOLATEY DATE CAKE: Fold in ½ cup (85g) of chopped bittersweet chocolate or chips just before you pour the batter into the pan.

Dress It Up

Serve slices of cake with Crème Fraîche Whip (page 180) or a scoop of vanilla ice cream.

chocolatey cakes

I love chocolate baked goods and there's nothing quite as satisfying as a fresh warm square of cake and a cold glass of milk.

This chapter is full of rich, chocolatey cakes that hit exactly that spot. They are packed with deep Dutch-process cocoa, lots of chopped chocolate, or both. Chocolate pairs beautifully with nutty, fruity, and spicy flavors, and in this collection of chocolatey treats you'll find all three—and some fun and unexpected pairings, too! There is a little something here for every type of chocolate lover.

Browned Butter, Pecan, and White Chocolate Cake

White chocolate has a reputation for being sugary-sweet and a little boring, but I've always had a soft spot for the good stuff where cocoa butter is a main ingredient. In this cake, toasty browned butter and pecans balance its creamy sweetness so well. If you can find caramelized white chocolate, like Valrhona Dulcey, I highly recommend giving it a try.

½ cup (113g) unsalted butter

¾ cup (150g) light brown sugar

2 large eggs

¾ cup (165g) plain whole-milk yogurt

1 teaspoon vanilla extract

½ teaspoon kosher salt

A few grates of nutmeg

1¼ cups (160g) all-purpose flour

1½ teaspoons baking powder

¼ teaspoon baking soda

¾ cup (75g) chopped toasted pecans

½ cup (85g) chopped white chocolate or white chocolate chips

1 tablespoon turbinado sugar

1. Position a rack in the center of your oven and preheat the oven to 350°F. Butter or coat an 8-inch square baking pan with nonstick spray. Line the pan with a strip of parchment paper that hangs over two of the edges.

2. **BROWN THE BUTTER:** Melt the butter in a small saucepan or skillet with a light-colored interior over medium heat. Cook the butter, stirring occasionally, scraping the bits from the bottom and sides of the pan if necessary, until the butter solids turn golden brown and smell nutty, about 3 minutes. Pour the butter into a large heatproof bowl and let it cool slightly.

3. Add the brown sugar and eggs to the warm butter and whisk until well-combined and foamy. Add the yogurt, vanilla, salt, and nutmeg. Whisk until smooth and emulsified.

4. Add the flour, baking powder, and baking soda and whisk until well-combined and smooth. Use a rubber spatula to fold in 6 tablespoons (37g) of the pecans and ¼ cup (42g) of the white chocolate.

recipe continues ⟶

5. Pour the batter into the prepared pan, tap the pan gently on the counter to release any air bubbles, and smooth the top of the batter with an offset spatula. Sprinkle the remaining 6 tablespoons (37g) pecans and remaining ¼ cup (42g) white chocolate over the batter. Finally, sprinkle the turbinado sugar over the top.

6. Bake the cake until puffed and golden, and a tester inserted into the center comes out clean, 30 to 40 minutes. Set the pan on a rack to cool for about 15 minutes. Then use the parchment paper to lift the cake out of the pan and set it on the rack to cool completely. (Store the cake, well wrapped, at room temperature for up to three days.)

Use Another Pan

LOAF: Bake in a 9 x 5 x 3-inch loaf pan until puffed and golden, and a skewer inserted into the center comes out clean, 35 to 45 minutes.

ROUND: Bake in a 9-inch round pan until puffed and golden, and a tester inserted into the center comes out clean, 30 to 40 minutes.

Flavor Variations

RASPBERRY WHITE CHOCOLATE CAKE: Fold in ½ cup (70g) fresh raspberries when you fold in the chocolate and pecans and sprinkle another ½ cup (70g) raspberries on top of the cake batter before you sprinkle on the remaining pecans and chocolate.

ROSEMARY, PECAN, AND WHITE CHOCOLATE CAKE: Add 1 tablespoon very finely chopped fresh rosemary when you add the vanilla and salt.

Dress It Up

Serve slices of cake with dollops of Brown Sugar Whip (page 180) and some shaved chocolate.

Cocoa Yogurt Cake

This is the most bang-for-your-buck chocolate cake I've ever made. It's delicious on its own, but there are lots of ways to top and transform it, too. I also have it on good authority that this cake is delicious the second day, warmed just a bit so the chocolatey bits melt slightly. Fold in any type of chocolate you like, but I like to really go for it with something bittersweet.

Cocoa Yogurt Cake

1 cup (200g) light brown sugar

2 large eggs

1 cup (220g) plain whole-milk yogurt

½ cup (120ml) neutral oil, like canola or grapeseed

1 teaspoon vanilla extract

¾ teaspoon kosher salt

¾ cup (68g) unsweetened Dutch-process cocoa powder

1 cup (128g) all-purpose flour

1 teaspoon baking powder

½ teaspoon baking soda

½ cup (85g) chopped chocolate or chocolate chips (optional)

Cocoa Glaze

1 cup (100g) confectioners' sugar

3 tablespoons unsweetened Dutch-process cocoa powder

1 tablespoon unsalted butter, very soft

Pinch of salt

2 to 3 tablespoons boiling water

1. Position a rack in the center of your oven and preheat the oven to 350°F. Butter or coat an 8-inch square baking pan with nonstick spray. Line the pan with a strip of parchment paper that hangs over two of the edges.

2. **MAKE THE CAKE:** In a large bowl, whisk the brown sugar and eggs until pale and foamy, about 1 minute. Add the yogurt, oil, vanilla, and salt. Whisk until smooth and emulsified. Add the cocoa powder and whisk until well-combined and smooth.

3. Add the flour, baking powder, and baking soda and whisk until well-combined and smooth. Fold in the chocolate, if using.

4. Pour the batter into the prepared pan, tap the pan gently on the counter to release any air bubbles, and smooth the top of the batter with an offset spatula.

5. Bake the cake until puffed and a tester inserted into the center comes out clean, 35 to 45 minutes. Set the cake on a rack to cool for about 15 minutes. Then use the parchment paper to lift the cake out of the pan and set it on the rack to cool completely.

recipe continues ⟶

6. **MAKE THE GLAZE:** Add the confectioners' sugar and cocoa to a bowl. Whisk until combined and any lumps in the cocoa have been broken up. Add the butter, salt, and 2 tablespoons boiling water and quickly whisk until smooth; if the glaze is very thick, add a few drops of water until it has a smooth and pourable consistency.

7. Immediately pour the glaze over the cooled cake (the glaze will harden to a more spreadable rather than pourable consistency if you let it sit). Let the glaze set for about 20 minutes before slicing the cake. (Store the cake, covered, at room temperature or in the fridge for up to three days.)

Flavor Variations

BERRY AND CHOCOLATE CAKE: Top the cake with Freeze-Dried Strawberry Glaze (page 75) and decorate with any combination of chopped pistachios, crushed freeze-dried berries, and shaved chocolate.

BLACK AND WHITE CAKE: Top the cake with Vanilla Bean Glaze (page 88) and sprinkle with chopped nuts or crushed freeze-dried berries for extra credit.

CHOCOLATE ESPRESSO CAKE: Make an espresso glaze by whisking 1 cup (100g) confectioners' sugar, 1 tablespoon instant espresso powder, a pinch of salt, and 1 to 2 tablespoons of milk to make a thick but pourable glaze. Pour the glaze over the cake while it is still just barely warm.

COCOA RYE CAKE: Substitute ½ cup (65g) light rye flour for an equal amount of the all-purpose flour.

Dress It Up

This cake is a great base for lots of flavors, so have fun! One option is to top slices of glazed or unglazed cake with ice cream, some Cocoa Whip (page 180), or Coffee Whip (page 180), and a sprinkle of chopped pistachios.

Use Another Pan

BUNDT: Double the ingredients for the cake and bake in a prepared 15-cup Bundt pan until puffed and a skewer inserted into the center comes out clean, 50 to 60 minutes. Let the cake cool in the pan for 10 minutes and then invert it onto a rack to cool completely. Double the ingredients for the glaze, too.

CUPCAKES: Bake in a cupcake tin lined with paper liners, filling them no more than halfway full, until puffed and a tester inserted into the center comes out clean, 12 to 18 minutes. Makes 12 to 18 cupcakes.

LOAF: Bake in a 9 x 5 x 3-inch loaf pan until puffed and a skewer inserted into the center comes out clean, 55 to 65 minutes. You'll need a half batch of glaze to coat the cake in a thin layer.

ROUND: Bake in a 9-inch round pan until puffed and a tester inserted into the center comes out clean, 35 to 45 minutes.

Use Another Pan

LOAF: Prepare the cake as directed, but instead of sprinkling 1 cup (140g) raspberries on top, fold ½ cup (70g) raspberries into the batter. Pour into a 9 x 5 x 3-inch loaf pan, then sprinkle ¼ cup (35g) raspberries over the top. Bake until puffed and a skewer inserted into the center comes out clean, 50 to 60 minutes.

ROUND: Bake in a 9-inch round pan until puffed and a tester inserted into the center comes out clean, 40 to 50 minutes.

Flavor Variations

CHOCOLATE-ALMOND OLIVE OIL CAKE WITH STRAWBERRIES: Substitute an equal amount of thinly sliced strawberries for the raspberries.

Dress It Up

Top slices of this cake with Fresh Berry Whip (made with raspberries; page 181) or scoops of ice cream and a sprinkle of chopped pistachios.

Chocolate-Almond
Olive Oil Cake with Raspberries

This fudgy chocolate cake is rich, dense, and not too sweet, thanks to the tart yogurt in the batter, a hefty dose of Dutch-process cocoa, and a sprinkle of fresh raspberries. The almond flour adds a lovely nubby texture, but you could certainly use all-purpose in its place.

1 cup (200g) sugar

2 large eggs

1 cup (220g) plain whole-milk yogurt

⅔ cup (160ml) olive oil

1 teaspoon vanilla extract

¾ teaspoon kosher salt

¾ cup (68g) unsweetened Dutch-process cocoa powder

¾ cup (95g) all-purpose flour

½ cup (55g) almond flour

1 teaspoon baking powder

½ teaspoon baking soda

1 cup (140g) fresh raspberries

1 tablespoon cacao nibs (optional)

1. Position a rack in the center of your oven and preheat the oven to 350°F. Butter or coat an 8-inch square baking pan with nonstick spray. Line the pan with a strip of parchment paper that hangs over two of the edges.

2. In a large bowl, whisk the sugar and eggs until pale and foamy, about 1 minute. Add the yogurt, oil, vanilla, and salt. Whisk until smooth and emulsified. Add the cocoa powder and whisk until well-combined and smooth.

3. Add the all-purpose flour, almond flour, baking powder, and baking soda and whisk until well-combined and smooth.

4. Pour the batter into the prepared pan, tap the pan gently on the counter to release any air bubbles, and smooth the top of the batter with an offset spatula. Scatter the raspberries and cacao nibs (if using) over the top.

5. Bake the cake until puffed and a tester inserted into the center comes out clean, 40 to 50 minutes. Set the pan on a rack to cool for about 15 minutes. Then use the parchment paper to lift the cake out of the pan and set it on the rack to cool completely. (Store this cake, well wrapped, in the fridge for up to three days. It has a very fudgy texture when cold. Yum!)

Minty Chocolate Malt Cake

Mint chocolate chip might be my very favorite ice cream flavor. Nothing beats a neon-green scoop on a warm summer evening, and yes, it must be green. The combination is rich and fresh all at once, and the addition of toasty malt powder here gives this cake an additional layer of flavor that you can't quite put your finger on unless you know it's there. Don't skip the silky chocolate mint glaze! It's not green, but you'll forgive me because it tastes so darn good.

Minty Chocolate Malt Cake

¾ cup (150g) light brown sugar

2 large eggs

½ cup (120ml) neutral oil, like canola or grapeseed

½ cup (120ml) whole milk

1 teaspoon vanilla extract

¾ teaspoon mint extract

¾ teaspoon kosher salt

½ cup (65g) malted milk powder

½ cup (45g) unsweetened Dutch-process cocoa powder

1 cup (128g) all-purpose flour

1 teaspoon baking powder

½ teaspoon baking soda

½ cup (120ml) hot coffee or water

1. Position a rack in the center of your oven and preheat the oven to 350°F. Butter or coat an 8-inch square baking pan with nonstick spray. Line the pan with a strip of parchment paper that hangs over two of the edges.

2. **MAKE THE CAKE:** In a large bowl, whisk the brown sugar and eggs until pale and foamy, about 1 minute. Add the oil, milk, vanilla, mint extract, and salt. Whisk until smooth and emulsified. Sift the malted milk powder and cocoa powder over the top and whisk them in.

3. Add the flour, baking powder, and baking soda and whisk until smooth. Lastly, add the coffee and stir until well-combined and smooth.

4. Pour the batter into the prepared pan, tap the pan gently on the counter to release any air bubbles, and smooth the top of the batter with an offset spatula.

recipe and ingredients continue $\longrightarrow$

Cocoa Mint Glaze

1 cup (100g) confectioners' sugar

3 tablespoons unsweetened Dutch-process cocoa powder

1 tablespoon unsalted butter, very soft

½ teaspoon mint extract

Pinch of salt

2 to 3 tablespoons boiling water

5. Bake the cake until puffed and a tester inserted into the center comes out clean, 30 to 40 minutes. Set the pan on a rack to cool for about 15 minutes. Then use the parchment paper to lift the cake out of the pan and set it on the rack to cool completely.

6. **MAKE THE GLAZE:** Add the confectioners' sugar and cocoa powder to a bowl. Whisk until combined and any lumps in the cocoa have been broken up. Add the butter, mint extract, salt, and 2 tablespoons boiling water and whisk until smooth. If the glaze is very thick, add a few drops of water until it is a smooth and pourable consistency.

7. Immediately pour the glaze over the cooled cake. If you let it sit, it gets fudgy and spreadable, rather than silky and pourable, which honestly isn't bad at all. Let the glaze set for about 20 minutes before slicing the cake. (Store the cake, covered, at room temperature for up to three days.)

Use Another Pan

LOAF: Bake in a 9 x 5 x 3-inch loaf pan until puffed and a skewer inserted into the center comes out clean, 50 to 60 minutes. You'll need a half batch of glaze to coat the cake in a thin layer.

ROUND: Bake in a 9-inch round pan until puffed and a tester inserted into the center comes out clean, 30 to 40 minutes.

SHEET: Double the ingredients for the cake and bake in a 9 x 13-inch pan until puffed and a tester inserted into the center comes out clean, 35 to 45 minutes. Double the ingredients for the glaze, too.

Dress It Up

This cake is a party on its own, but a little bit of Cocoa Whip (page 180) served alongside slices of cake would be lovely.

Chocolate-Orange Beet Cake

I know this seems like a wild combination, but earthy, sweet beets and chocolate are a surprisingly great pair, and the orange really ties it all together. We're using beets twice here, once to add flavor, texture, and moisture to this orangey chocolate cake and again to tint and gently flavor the glaze. Use the large holes of a box grater to shred the beets for the cake, and a fine grater like a Microplane to prepare the beets for the glaze. The poppy seeds are optional, but I love the crunch, so toss some in if you keep them in your pantry.

Chocolate-Orange Beet Cake

1 small orange

¾ cup (150g) granulated sugar

2 large eggs

½ cup (110g) sour cream

½ cup (120ml) neutral oil, like canola or grapeseed

1 teaspoon vanilla extract

¾ teaspoon kosher salt

½ cup (45g) unsweetened Dutch-process cocoa powder

1 cup (128g) all-purpose flour

2 teaspoons baking powder

¼ teaspoon baking soda

2 cups (165g) grated peeled red beets, loosely packed

1 tablespoon poppy seeds (optional)

1. Position a rack in the center of your oven and preheat the oven to 350°F. Butter or coat an 8-inch square baking pan with nonstick spray. Line the pan with a strip of parchment paper that hangs over two of the edges.

2. **MAKE THE CAKE:** Zest the orange into a large bowl and add the sugar and eggs. Whisk until pale and foamy, about 1 minute. Add the sour cream, oil, vanilla, and salt. Whisk until smooth and emulsified. Add the cocoa powder and whisk until smooth.

3. Add the flour, baking powder, and baking soda and whisk until well-combined and smooth. Finally, use a rubber spatula to fold in the beets and poppy seeds (if using).

4. Pour the batter into the prepared pan, tap the pan gently on the counter to release any air bubbles, and smooth the top of the batter with an offset spatula.

recipe and ingredients continue ⟶

1¼ cups (125g) confectioners' sugar, or more as needed

½ teaspoon orange zest

1 tablespoon finely grated red beet

1 tablespoon fresh orange juice, or more as needed

Pinch of salt

Poppy seeds, to finish (optional)

5. Bake the cake until puffed and a tester inserted into the center comes out clean, 35 to 45 minutes. Set the pan on a rack to cool for about 15 minutes. Then use the parchment paper to lift the cake out of the pan and set it on the rack to cool completely.

6. **MAKE THE GLAZE:** Add the confectioners' sugar, grated beet, orange juice, orange zest, and salt to a bowl and whisk until smooth. The glaze should be very thick. If it is too thin, add a bit more confectioners' sugar until you achieve a pourable consistency. If it is too thick, add a few more drops of orange juice. Pour the glaze over the cooled cake and sprinkle with the additional poppy seeds, if desired. (Store the cake, covered, at room temperature for up to three days. The glaze will soften over time.)

Use Another Pan

LOAF: Bake in a 9 x 5 x 3-inch loaf pan until puffed and a skewer inserted into the center comes out clean, 45 to 55 minutes. You'll need a half batch of glaze to coat the cake in a thin layer.

ROUND: Bake in a 9-inch round pan until puffed and a tester inserted into the center comes out clean, 35 to 45 minutes.

Flavor Variations

DOUBLE CHOCOLATE BEET CAKE: Omit the Beet and Orange Glaze and top the cake with Cocoa Glaze (page 135) instead.

Dress It Up

Serve slices of cake with Cocoa Whip (page 180) and some chopped toasted nuts. A scoop of chocolate ice cream wouldn't be out of place, either.

Use Another Pan

BUNDT: Double the ingredients for the cake and bake in a prepared 15-cup Bundt pan until puffed and a skewer inserted into the center comes out clean, 55 to 65 minutes. Let the cake cool in the pan for 15 minutes, then invert it onto a rack to cool completely.

LOAF: Bake in a 9 x 5 x 3-inch loaf pan until puffed and a skewer inserted into the center comes out clean, 50 to 60 minutes.

ROUND: Bake in a 9-inch round pan until puffed and a tester inserted into the center comes out clean, 35 to 45 minutes.

Flavor Variations

WHOLE WHEAT CHOCOLATE AND ZUCCHINI CAKE: Substitute ½ cup (65g) whole wheat flour for an equal amount of the all-purpose flour.

Dress It Up

Serve slices of cake with caramel, chocolate, or vanilla ice cream or a dollop of Cocoa Whip (page 180).

Chocolate and Zucchini Cake

Sure, the zucchini in this cake adds some nutritional value, but more important, it lends a wonderful soft texture to the crumb. The poppy seeds add some crunch, and the chopped chocolate ensures it doesn't taste too wholesome. I think this cake is great on its own, but if you'd like to add a topping, I suggest the Cocoa Glaze (page 135).

¾ cup (150g) sugar

2 large eggs

¾ cup (180ml) neutral oil, like canola or grapeseed

1 tablespoon poppy seeds (optional)

½ teaspoon cardamom

¼ teaspoon cinnamon

¾ teaspoon kosher salt

½ cup (45g) unsweetened Dutch-process cocoa powder

1¼ cups (160g) all-purpose flour

½ teaspoon baking powder

½ teaspoon baking soda

2¼ cups (225g) grated zucchini (use large holes of a box grater), squeezed to remove excess moisture

¾ cup (128g) chopped bittersweet or semisweet chocolate or chocolate chips

1. Position a rack in the center of your oven and preheat the oven to 350°F. Butter or coat an 8-inch square baking pan with nonstick spray. Line the pan with a strip of parchment paper that hangs over two of the edges.

2. In a large bowl, whisk the sugar and eggs until pale and foamy, about 1 minute. Add the oil, poppy seeds (if using), cardamom, cinnamon, and salt. Whisk until smooth and emulsified. Add the cocoa powder and whisk until smooth.

3. Add the flour, baking powder, and baking soda and stir until well-combined and smooth. Use a rubber spatula to fold in the grated zucchini and ½ cup (85g) of the chocolate.

4. Pour the batter into the prepared pan, tap the pan gently on the counter to release any air bubbles, and smooth the top of the batter with an offset spatula. Sprinkle the remaining ¼ cup (42g) chocolate over the top of the cake.

5. Bake the cake until puffed and a tester inserted into the center comes out clean, 35 to 45 minutes. Set the pan on a rack to cool for about 15 minutes. Then use the parchment paper to lift the cake out of the pan and set it on the rack to cool completely. (Store the cake, well wrapped, at room temperature for up to three days.)

Espresso Chocolate Chip Cake

This cake is a serious pick-me-up, packed with a hefty dose of espresso and lots and lots of chocolate chips. It also, very charmingly, looks like a giant chocolate chip cookie. Use any type of chocolate you like; a mix of milk and bittersweet is my personal favorite.

¾ cup (150g) plus 1 tablespoon sugar

2 large eggs

1 cup (220g) whole-milk ricotta

½ cup (120ml) neutral oil, like canola or grapeseed

4 teaspoons instant espresso powder, dissolved in 2 tablespoons very hot water

2 teaspoons vanilla bean paste or vanilla extract

¾ teaspoon kosher salt

1¼ cups (160g) all-purpose flour

1½ teaspoons baking powder

½ teaspoon baking soda

1 cup (170g) chocolate chips (any type you like)

1. Position a rack in the center of your oven and preheat the oven to 350°F. Butter or coat an 8-inch square baking pan with nonstick spray. Line the pan with a strip of parchment paper that hangs over two of the edges.

2. In a large bowl, whisk ¾ cup (150g) of the sugar and the eggs until pale and foamy, about 1 minute. Add the ricotta, oil, espresso, vanilla, and salt. Whisk until smooth and emulsified.

3. Add the flour, baking powder, and baking soda to the bowl. Whisk until well-combined and smooth. Use a rubber spatula to fold in ½ cup (85g) of the chocolate chips.

4. Pour the batter into the prepared pan, tap the pan gently on the counter to release any air bubbles, and smooth the top of the batter with an offset spatula. Scatter the remaining ½ cup (85g) chocolate chips over the top and sprinkle with the remaining tablespoon sugar.

5. Bake the cake until puffed and a tester inserted into the center comes out clean, 35 to 45 minutes. Set the cake on a rack to cool for about 15 minutes. Then use the parchment paper to lift the cake out of the pan and set it on the rack to cool completely. (Store the cake, well wrapped, at room temperature for up to three days.)

Use Another Pan

LOAF: Fold ¾ cup (128g) chocolate chips into the batter, and sprinkle ¼ cup (42g) over the top. Bake in a 9 x 5 x 3-inch loaf pan until puffed and a skewer inserted into the center comes out clean, 50 to 60 minutes.

ROUND: Bake in a 9-inch round pan until puffed and a tester inserted into the center comes out clean, 30 to 40 minutes.

Flavor Variations

BANANA ESPRESSO CHOCOLATE CHIP CAKE: Substitute ½ cup (115g) mashed banana for ½ cup (110g) of the ricotta.

MOCHA ALMOND CAKE: Fold in ¼ cup (55g) almond paste, broken into small pieces, along with the chocolate chips. Bake the cake as directed and cool on a rack. Make a batch of Cocoa Glaze (page 135) and whisk in ½ teaspoon almond extract. Pour the glaze on the cooled cake and top with ½ cup (50g) sliced almonds.

Dress It Up

Top slices of cake with Whipped Vanilla Mascarpone (page 182) and a light dusting of cocoa powder for a tiramisu vibe.

Chocolate Peanut Butter Cake

There is a lot to love about this classic combination. Deep chocolate cake is infused with a generous amount of smooth, salty peanut butter (something like Skippy is ideal here), then covered with a thin layer of peanut butter glaze. Top the whole thing with some chopped roasted peanuts, and don't forget to pour yourself a glass of milk. If you really want to gild the lily, fold ½ cup (85g) of peanut butter chips into the batter just before pouring it into the pan.

Chocolate Peanut Butter Cake

1 cup (200g) light brown sugar

2 large eggs

½ cup (125g) smooth peanut butter

½ cup (120ml) neutral oil, like canola or grapeseed

½ cup (120ml) whole milk

1 teaspoon vanilla extract

¾ teaspoon kosher salt

½ cup (45g) unsweetened Dutch-process cocoa powder

1 cup (128g) all-purpose flour

1 teaspoon baking powder

½ teaspoon baking soda

½ cup (120ml) hot coffee or water

1. Position a rack in the center of your oven and preheat the oven to 350°F. Butter or coat an 8-inch square baking pan with nonstick spray. Line the pan with a strip of parchment paper that hangs over two of the edges.

2. **MAKE THE CAKE:** In a large bowl, whisk the brown sugar and eggs until pale and foamy, about 1 minute. Add the peanut butter, oil, milk, vanilla, and kosher salt. Whisk the mixture until smooth and emulsified. Add the cocoa powder and whisk until smooth.

3. Add the flour, baking powder, and baking soda and whisk until well-combined and smooth. Lastly, add the coffee and stir until well-combined and smooth.

4. Pour the batter into the prepared pan, tap the pan gently on the counter to release any air bubbles, and smooth the top of the batter with an offset spatula.

5. Bake the cake until puffed and a tester inserted into the center comes out clean, 45 to 55 minutes. Set the cake on a rack to cool for about 15 minutes. Then use the parchment paper to lift the cake out of the pan and set it on the rack to cool completely.

recipe and ingredients continue ⟶

Peanut Butter Glaze

1 cup (100g) confectioners' sugar

2 tablespoons smooth peanut butter

1 teaspoon vanilla extract

Pinch of salt

1 to 2 tablespoons hot water

½ cup (55g) chopped roasted and salted peanuts

Flaky salt, to finish (optional)

6. **MAKE THE GLAZE:** In a bowl, whisk the confectioners' sugar, peanut butter, vanilla, kosher salt, and 1 tablespoon hot water until smooth. If the glaze is very thick, add more water, a few drops at a time, until it is a smooth and pourable consistency.

7. Pour the glaze over the cooled cake and sprinkle with chopped peanuts and a few sprinkles of flaky salt (if using). Let the glaze set for about 20 minutes before slicing the cake. (Store the cake, well-covered, at room temperature for up to three days.)

Use Another Pan

LOAF: Bake in a 9 x 5 x 3-inch loaf pan until puffed and a skewer inserted into the center comes out clean, 55 to 65 minutes. You'll need a half batch of glaze to coat the cake in a thin layer.

ROUND: Bake in a 9-inch round pan until puffed and a tester inserted into the center comes out clean, 45 to 55 minutes.

Dress It Up

Top slices of cake with Cocoa Whip (page 180) and mini peanut butter cups. Yeah, that's right, I said to top a cake with peanut butter cups.

Use Another Pan

LOAF: Pour the batter into a 9 x 5 x 3-inch loaf pan. Top the batter with 2 tablespoons chopped hazelnuts instead of ¼ cup. Bake until puffed and a skewer inserted into the center comes out clean, 50 to 60 minutes.

ROUND: Bake in a 9-inch round pan until puffed and a tester inserted into the center comes out clean, 40 to 50 minutes.

Dress It Up

Serve slices of cake with Cocoa Whip (page 180) and chopped toasted hazelnuts. A scoop of vanilla or chocolate ice cream wouldn't be out of place, either.

Milk Chocolate Chip-Hazelnut Cake

I had somehow managed to miss out on the magic of Nutella for the first twenty years of my life, but when I studied abroad in Spain, my host family served it for breakfast every day. It felt very sneaky to eat warm, creamy chocolate spread on toast first thing in the morning. This cocoa cake is a little more decadent than a slice of Bimbo bread, and the combination of milk chocolate and toasty hazelnuts is as good as ever.

¾ cup (150g) sugar

1 large egg

½ cup (160g) chocolate hazelnut spread, like Nutella

½ cup (120ml) neutral oil, like canola or grapeseed

½ cup (120ml) whole milk

1 teaspoon vanilla extract

¾ teaspoon kosher salt

½ cup (45g) unsweetened Dutch-process cocoa powder

1 cup (128g) all-purpose flour

1 teaspoon baking powder

½ teaspoon baking soda

¼ cup (60ml) hot coffee or water

¼ cup (40g) chocolate chips or chopped milk chocolate

¼ cup (30g) finely chopped hazelnuts

1. Position a rack in the center of your oven and preheat the oven to 350°F. Butter or coat an 8-inch square baking pan with nonstick spray. Line the pan with a strip of parchment paper that hangs over two of the edges.

2. In a large bowl, whisk the sugar and egg until pale and foamy, about 1 minute. Add the chocolate hazelnut spread, oil, milk, vanilla, and salt. Whisk until smooth and emulsified. Add the cocoa powder and whisk until smooth.

3. Add the flour, baking powder, and baking soda and whisk until well-combined and smooth. Stir in the coffee, then fold in the chocolate.

4. Pour the batter into the prepared pan, tap the pan gently on the counter to release any air bubbles, and smooth the top with an offset spatula. Scatter the chopped hazelnuts over the top.

5. Bake the cake until puffed and a tester inserted into the center comes out clean, 40 to 50 minutes. Set the pan on a rack to cool for about 15 minutes. Then use the parchment paper to lift the cake out of the pan and set it on the rack to cool completely. (Store the cake, well wrapped, at room temperature for up to three days.)

Red Velvet Cake
with Cream Cheese Glaze

When you're in the mood for something chocolatey but not too rich, this classic cake made snackable is the perfect thing to throw together. Instead of traditional cream cheese frosting, the cake is coated in a layer of tangy cream cheese glaze, making it a little less dessert and a little more afternoon treat. Use gel food coloring for the most vibrant color; natural dyes will be a bit muted.

Red Velvet Cake

¾ cup (150g) sugar

1 large egg

¾ cup (180ml) buttermilk, well shaken

½ cup (120ml) neutral oil, like canola or grapeseed

1 teaspoon vanilla extract

¾ teaspoon kosher salt

½ teaspoon red gel food coloring

¼ cup (23g) unsweetened Dutch-process cocoa powder

1¼ cups (160g) all-purpose flour

1 teaspoon baking powder

½ teaspoon baking soda

Cream Cheese Glaze

1 cup (100g) confectioners' sugar

2 tablespoons cream cheese

2 to 3 tablespoons whole milk

½ teaspoon vanilla bean paste or vanilla extract

Pinch of salt

1.   Position a rack in the center of your oven and preheat the oven to 350°F. Butter or coat an 8-inch square baking pan with nonstick spray. Line the pan with a strip of parchment paper that hangs over two of the edges.

2.   **MAKE THE CAKE:** In a large bowl, whisk the sugar and egg until pale and foamy, about 1 minute. Add the buttermilk, oil, vanilla, salt, and food coloring. Whisk until smooth and emulsified. Add the cocoa powder and whisk until smooth.

3.   Add the flour, baking powder, and baking soda and whisk until well-combined and smooth.

4.   Pour the batter into the pan, tap the pan gently on the counter to release any air bubbles, and smooth the top of the batter with an offset spatula.

5.   Bake the cake until puffed and a tester inserted into the center comes out clean, 25 to 35 minutes. Set the pan on a rack to cool for about 15 minutes. Then use the parchment paper to lift the cake out of the pan and set it on the rack to cool completely.

recipe continues ⟶

6. **MAKE THE GLAZE:** Add the confectioners' sugar, cream cheese, 2 tablespoons milk, vanilla paste, and salt to a bowl and carefully whisk until smooth. Stir slowly at first, just to moisten the sugar, then whisk more vigorously until the glaze is smooth. Add a bit more milk, if needed, to make a smooth, thick glaze.

7. Pour the glaze over the cooled cake and let it set for about 20 minutes before slicing the cake. (Store the cake, covered, at room temperature for up to three days.)

Use Another Pan

CUPCAKES: Bake in a cupcake tin lined with paper liners, filling them no more than halfway full, until puffed and a tester inserted into the center comes out clean, 12 to 18 minutes. Makes 12 to 18 cupcakes.

LOAF: Bake in a 9 x 5 x 3-inch loaf pan until puffed and a skewer inserted into the center comes out clean, 40 to 50 minutes. You'll need a half batch of glaze to coat the cake in a thin layer.

ROUND: Bake in a 9-inch round pan until puffed and a tester inserted into the center comes out clean, 25 to 35 minutes.

SHEET: Double the ingredients for the cake and bake in a 9 x 13-inch pan until puffed and a tester inserted into the center comes out clean, 30 to 40 minutes. Double the ingredients for the glaze, too.

Flavor Variations

This cake is also delicious topped with Cocoa Glaze (page 135).

Dress It Up

Serve slices of cake with Crème Fraîche Whip (page 180) instead of the glaze or use both!

Spiced Chocolate Pumpkin Cake

This lightly spiced chocolate cake is packed with pumpkin puree, and has just a pinch of cayenne for a pleasing bit of unexpected warmth. If you'd like to omit the spiced pumpkin glaze, top the cake with 2 tablespoons granulated sugar mixed with ½ teaspoon ground cinnamon and another tiny pinch of cayenne instead. Halve the sugar-spice mixture for a loaf cake.

Spiced Chocolate Pumpkin Cake

¾ cup (150g) light brown sugar

2 large eggs

1 cup (230g) pumpkin puree

½ cup (120ml) olive oil

½ cup (120ml) whole milk

1 teaspoon vanilla extract

1 teaspoon ground cinnamon

½ teaspoon kosher salt

Pinch of cayenne (optional)

½ cup (45g) unsweetened Dutch-process cocoa powder

1 cup (128g) all-purpose flour

1 teaspoon baking powder

½ teaspoon baking soda

½ cup (85g) chopped chocolate or chocolate chips

1. Position a rack in the center of your oven and preheat the oven to 350°F. Butter or coat an 8-inch square baking pan with nonstick spray. Line the pan with a strip of parchment paper that hangs over two of the edges.

2. **MAKE THE CAKE:** In a large bowl, whisk the brown sugar and eggs until pale and foamy, about 1 minute. Add the pumpkin puree, oil, milk, vanilla, cinnamon, salt, and cayenne (if using). Whisk until smooth and emulsified. Add the cocoa powder and whisk until smooth.

3. Add the flour, baking powder, and baking soda and whisk until well-combined and smooth. Fold in the chocolate with a rubber spatula.

4. Pour the batter into the prepared pan, tap the pan gently on the counter to release any air bubbles, and smooth the top of the batter with an offset spatula.

5. Bake the cake until puffed and a tester inserted into the center comes out clean, 45 to 55 minutes. Set the cake on a rack to cool for about 15 minutes. Then use the parchment paper to lift the cake out of the pan and set it on the rack to cool completely.

recipe and ingredients continue ⟶

Spiced Pumpkin Glaze

1 cup (100g) confectioners' sugar

1 tablespoon pumpkin puree

1 tablespoon whole milk, or more as needed

¼ teaspoon ground cinnamon

Pinch of cayenne (optional)

Pinch of ground cloves

Pinch of salt

6. **MAKE THE GLAZE:** In a bowl, whisk the confectioners' sugar, pumpkin, milk, cinnamon, cayenne (if using), cloves, and salt until smooth. If the glaze is very thick, add a few drops of milk until it is a smooth and pourable consistency.

7. Pour the glaze over the cooled cake and let it set for about 20 minutes before slicing the cake. (Store the cake, covered, at room temperature for up to three days.)

Use Another Pan

LOAF: Bake in a 9 x 5 x 3-inch loaf pan until puffed and a skewer inserted into the center comes out clean, 55 to 65 minutes.

ROUND: Bake in a 9-inch round pan until puffed and a tester inserted into the center comes out clean, 45 to 55 minutes.

Flavor Variations

Try this cake topped with shiny Cocoa Glaze (page 135) instead of the pumpkin glaze. A handful of chopped, toasted nuts wouldn't be out of place, either.

Dress It Up

Top slices of cake with Cocoa Whip (page 180) or scoops of chocolate ice cream and Whiskey Caramel (page 126).

Fudgy Chocolate Cake
with Fluffy Chocolate Frosting

This cake is dense, fudgy, and super chocolatey. The buttercream frosting pushes it directly into dessert territory, but sometimes you just need a fluffy frosting cap on your cake to turn your day around. This frosting is one of the few times in this book you'll have to pull out a hand mixer, but if that's not your speed, try the Cocoa Glaze (page 135) instead.

Fudgy Chocolate Cake

1 cup (200g) granulated sugar

2 large eggs

1 cup (240ml) buttermilk, well shaken

¼ cup (60ml) neutral oil, like canola or grapeseed

¼ cup (55g) unsalted butter, melted

1 teaspoon vanilla extract

¾ teaspoon kosher salt

¾ cup (68g) unsweetened Dutch-process cocoa powder

1 cup (128g) all-purpose flour

1 teaspoon baking powder

½ teaspoon baking soda

¼ cup (60ml) hot coffee or water

⅓ cup (55g) chopped bittersweet chocolate or chocolate chips (optional)

1. Position a rack in the center of your oven and preheat the oven to 350°F. Butter or coat an 8-inch square baking pan with nonstick spray. Line the pan with a strip of parchment paper that hangs over two of the edges.

2. **MAKE THE CAKE:** In a large bowl, whisk the sugar and eggs until pale and foamy, about 1 minute. Add the buttermilk, oil, butter, vanilla, and salt. Whisk until smooth and emulsified. Add the cocoa powder and whisk until smooth.

3. Add the flour, baking powder, and baking soda and whisk until well-combined and smooth. Gently stir in the coffee, then fold in the chocolate (if using).

4. Pour the batter into the prepared pan, tap the pan gently on the counter to release any air bubbles, and smooth the top of the batter with an offset spatula.

5. Bake the cake until puffed and a tester inserted into the center comes out clean, 35 to 45 minutes. Set the pan on a rack to cool for about 15 minutes. Then use the parchment paper to lift the cake out of the pan and set it on the rack to cool completely.

Fluffy Chocolate Frosting

6 tablespoons (85g) unsalted butter, very soft

¼ cup (23g) unsweetened Dutch-process cocoa powder

1 cup (100g) confectioners' sugar

1 teaspoon vanilla extract

Pinch of salt

2 to 3 tablespoons milk

Shaved chocolate or sprinkles, to finish

6. **MAKE THE FROSTING:** Add the butter to a large bowl and mix with an electric mixer on medium-high until smooth and creamy. Turn the mixer to low, add the cocoa powder, and mix until smooth, scraping the bottom and sides of the bowl as necessary, then slowly add the confectioners' sugar. Mix until the sugar is moistened, then add the vanilla, a pinch of salt, and 2 tablespoons milk. Turn the mixer to medium high and whip until light and fluffy, adding more milk as necessary to make a smooth and fluffy frosting.

7. Top the cooled cake with swoops of frosting and scatter the shaved chocolate or sprinkles over the top. (Store the cake, covered, at room temperature or in the fridge for up to three days.)

Use Another Pan

LOAF: Bake in a 9 x 5 x 3-inch loaf pan until puffed and a skewer inserted into the center comes out clean, 50 to 60 minutes.

ROUND: Bake in a 9-inch round pan until puffed and a tester inserted into the center comes out clean, 35 to 45 minutes.

SHEET: Double the ingredients for the cake and bake in a 9 x 13-inch pan until puffed and a tester inserted into the center comes out clean, 40 to 50 minutes. Double the ingredients for the frosting, too.

Flavor Variations

Top the cooled cake with Fluffy Vanilla Frosting (page 173) or Fluffy Strawberry Frosting (page 174) instead of the chocolate frosting.

CHOCOLATE TURTLE CAKE: Fold ½ cup (65g) finely chopped toasted pecans into the batter (save a tablespoon or two to sprinkle on top of the cake) along with the chocolate chips. Bake as directed, then let the cake cool. Top slices of cake with warm Whiskey Caramel (page 126).

Dress It Up

Serve slices of cake with ice cream if you really want to take this cake to party-town.

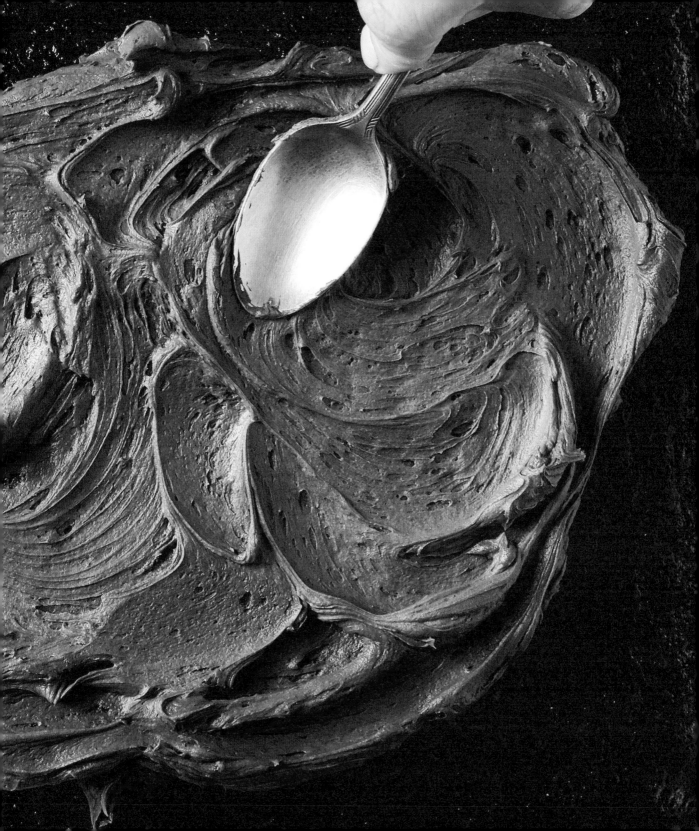

Vegan Chocolate Coconut Cake

This dairy- and egg-free cake isn't short on richness or flavor, thanks to lots of coconut milk and coconut oil. You can use refined or unrefined coconut oil interchangeably in this recipe, although unrefined has more coconut flavor. This cake is quite light and delicate, so let it cool completely before attempting to slice it.

1 cup (240ml) full-fat coconut milk, well stirred

¾ cup (150g) sugar

½ cup (120ml) coconut oil, melted

¼ cup (60ml) hot water

1 tablespoon apple cider vinegar or distilled white vinegar

1 teaspoon coconut extract (optional)

1 teaspoon vanilla extract

1 teaspoon instant espresso powder (optional)

¾ teaspoon kosher salt

½ cup (45g) unsweetened Dutch-process cocoa powder

1¼ cups (160g) all-purpose flour

1 teaspoon baking powder

½ teaspoon baking soda

½ cup (85g) vegan chocolate chips

⅔ cup (30g) unsweetened flaked coconut

1. Position a rack in the center of your oven and preheat the oven to 350°F. Spray an 8-inch square baking pan with nonstick spray. Line the pan with a strip of parchment paper that hangs over two of the edges.

2. In a large bowl, whisk the coconut milk, sugar, coconut oil, water, vinegar, coconut extract (if using), vanilla, instant espresso powder (if using), and salt until smooth and emulsified. Sift the cocoa powder over the top and whisk it in.

3. Add the flour, baking powder, and baking soda and whisk until just smooth. Use the edge of the whisk to scrape the bottom and sides of the bowl to ensure even mixing. Fold in ¼ cup (42g) of the chocolate chips.

4. Pour the batter into the prepared pan, tap the pan gently on the counter to release any air bubbles, and smooth the top of the batter with an offset spatula. Sprinkle the top of the batter with the remaining ¼ cup (42g) chocolate chips and the coconut flakes.

5. Bake the cake until puffed and a tester inserted into the center comes out clean or with a bit of melted chocolate from the chips, 25 to 35 minutes. Set the cake on a rack to cool for about 15 minutes. Then use the parchment paper to lift the cake out of the pan and set it on the rack to cool completely. (Store the cake, well wrapped, at room temperature or in the fridge for up to three days.)

Use Another Pan

LOAF: Sprinkle ⅓ cup (15g) flaked coconut over the top of the batter in a 9 x 5 x 3-inch loaf pan and bake until puffed and a tester inserted into the center comes out clean, 45 to 55 minutes. If the coconut on top starts to brown before the cake is cooked through, tent the cake with aluminum foil.

ROUND: Bake in a 9-inch round pan until puffed and a tester inserted into the center comes out clean, 25 to 35 minutes.

Flavor Variations

RASPBERRY CHOCOLATE COCONUT CAKE:
Sprinkle 1 cup (140g) fresh raspberries over the top of the batter before adding the coconut flakes.

not your
average
vanilla cakes

Vanilla has a special place in the baking pantry because it helps enhance so many other flavors, yet also stands beautifully on its own. These vanilla cakes highlight one of my very favorite sweet, floral flavors, and they also give it a few fun twists. If you can swing it, splurge on a little bottle of vanilla bean paste—those little flecks of vanilla make these cakes feel extra special. Nielsen Massey and Heilala both make delicious high-quality vanilla extracts and paste.

Vanilla Buttermilk Cake
with Fluffy Vanilla Frosting

Folks, this is the closest thing to a yellow cake from a boxed mix that I've ever made in my home kitchen—and that's a good thing! You'll want to break out your vanilla bean paste for this soft vanilla-packed cake. It's also easy to dress this cake up for pretty much any occasion. I've included instructions for making it rainbow sprinkley, malty, and extra golden in the variations.

Vanilla Buttermilk Cake

¾ cup (150g) granulated sugar

1 large egg

1 cup (240ml) buttermilk, well shaken

¼ cup (55g) unsalted butter, melted

¼ cup (60ml) neutral oil, like canola or grapeseed

2 teaspoons vanilla bean paste or vanilla extract

½ teaspoon kosher salt

1¼ cups (160g) all-purpose flour

1 teaspoon baking powder

½ teaspoon baking soda

Fluffy Vanilla Frosting

1 cup (100g) confectioners' sugar

¼ cup (55g) unsalted butter, very soft

1 tablespoon milk, or more as needed

2 teaspoons vanilla bean paste or vanilla extract

1 teaspoon lemon juice

Pinch of salt

Sprinkles (optional)

1. Position a rack in the center of your oven and preheat the oven to 350°F. Butter or coat an 8-inch square baking pan with nonstick spray. Line the pan with a strip of parchment paper that hangs over two of the edges.

2. MAKE THE CAKE: In a large bowl, whisk the sugar and egg until pale and foamy, about 1 minute. Add the buttermilk, butter, oil, vanilla, and salt. Whisk until smooth and emulsified.

3. Add the flour, baking powder, and baking soda and whisk until well-combined and smooth.

4. Pour the batter into the prepared pan, tap the pan gently on the counter to release any air bubbles, and smooth the top of the batter with an offset spatula.

5. Bake the cake until puffed and golden, and a tester inserted into the center comes out clean, 30 to 40 minutes. Set the pan on a rack to cool for about 15 minutes. Then use the parchment paper to lift the cake out of the pan and set it on the rack to cool completely.

recipe continues ⟶

6. **MAKE THE FROSTING:** Add the confectioners' sugar, butter, milk, vanilla, lemon juice, and salt to a large bowl. Use an electric hand mixer to mix the ingredients on low until the sugar is moistened. Use a rubber spatula to scrape down the sides of the bowl as necessary. Mix until the ingredients are combined, then turn the mixer up to medium high and whip until light and fluffy, about 2 minutes, adding a bit more milk, if necessary, to make a smooth, fluffy frosting.

7. Top the cooled cake with swoops and swirls of frosting and sprinkles if you like. (Store the cake, loosely covered, at room temperature or in the fridge for up to three days.)

Use Another Pan

CUPCAKES: Bake in a cupcake tin lined with paper liners, filling them no more than halfway full, until puffed and golden, and a tester inserted into the center comes out clean, 12 to 18 minutes. Makes 12 to 18 cupcakes. (These cupcakes will have flat rather than domed tops.)

ROUND: Bake in a 9-inch round pan until puffed and golden, and a tester inserted into the center comes out clean, 30 to 40 minutes.

SHEET: Double the ingredients for the cake and bake in a 9 x 13-inch pan until puffed and golden, and a tester inserted into the center comes out clean, 35 to 45 minutes. Double the ingredients for the frosting, too.

Flavor Variations

GOLDEN VANILLA CAKE: Whisk in ½ teaspoon ground turmeric with the vanilla bean paste for a beautifully golden cake. Top with Lemon Glaze (page 44).

RAINBOW SPRINKLE CAKE: Fold in 2 tablespoons of rainbow sprinkles (the long cylindrical type, not the round type) when you add the flour. For that birthday-cake-from-a-boxed-mix flavor, substitute 1 teaspoon imitation vanilla extract for the vanilla bean paste in both the cake and frosting. Spread the frosting over the cooled cake in swoops and swirls, and top with more sprinkles.

MALTED VANILLA CAKE: Add ¼ cup (28g) malt powder when you add the flour to the mix for a deeper milky flavor. If necessary, sift the malt powder to ensure that it is smooth and not at all lumpy when you add it to the batter.

STRAWBERRY FROSTED VANILLA CAKE: For Fluffy Strawberry Frosting, prepare the Fluffy Vanilla Frosting but leave out the vanilla and add ¼ cup (7g) crushed freeze-dried strawberries along with the confectioners' sugar. Top the cake with sliced fresh strawberries or a sprinkle of freeze-dried strawberries, if desired.

Dress It Up

Dress up this cake for a party by topping it with Fresh Berry Whip (page 181), vanilla ice cream, and fresh fruit.

SNACKING CAKES

174

put some whipped cream on it

Billowy whipped cream is just about the best thing to pair with any of these cakes to make them feel extra special. I always like to whip cream by hand so I can control the texture, and when you're making a small amount, as in these recipes, it doesn't take long. Start with very cold heavy cream, a large bowl so the cream has lots of room to move, and a balloon-style whisk, and you'll have whipped cream in a couple of minutes flat. If your arm gets tired, you can always pass the bowl to a friend to help out. You can use a hand mixer, too. Just don't overwhip! You are looking for soft, dreamy peaks. Whip your cream just before you plan to serve it.

Brown Sugar Whip

Molasses-y and sweet

MAKES ABOUT 2 CUPS

1 cup (240ml) chilled heavy cream

2 tablespoons dark brown sugar or muscovado sugar

Add the cream and brown sugar to a large bowl. Whisk to soft peaks and serve immediately.

Cocoa Whip

Rich and chocolatey

MAKES ABOUT 2 CUPS

2 tablespoons unsweetened Dutch-process cocoa powder

4 teaspoons sugar

1 cup (240ml) chilled heavy cream

Add the cocoa and sugar to a large bowl and whisk until all of the lumps in the cocoa have been broken up. Add the cream, whisk to soft peaks, and serve immediately.

Coffee Whip

Toasty and bittersweet

MAKES ABOUT 2 CUPS

1 cup (240ml) chilled heavy cream

1 tablespoon sugar

1 teaspoon instant espresso powder

Add the cream, sugar, and espresso powder to a large bowl. Whisk to soft peaks and serve immediately.

Crème Fraîche Whip

Cultured and tart

MAKES ABOUT 2 CUPS

1 cup (240ml) chilled heavy cream

2 tablespoons crème fraîche

4 teaspoons sugar

Add the cream, crème fraîche, and sugar to a large bowl. Whisk to soft peaks and serve immediately.

Freeze-Dried Fruit Whip

Fruity and fun

MAKES ABOUT 2 CUPS

2 tablespoons crushed freeze-dried fruit, such as strawberries or raspberries

1 tablespoon sugar

1 cup (240ml) chilled heavy cream

Add the fruit and sugar to a large bowl and whisk to combine. Add the cream, whisk to soft peaks, and serve immediately.

Fresh Berry Whip

Tart and fresh

MAKES ABOUT 2 CUPS

¼ cup fresh strawberries or raspberries

4 teaspoons sugar

1 cup (240ml) chilled heavy cream

1. In a small bowl, combine the berries with 1 teaspoon of the sugar and mash them with a fork.

2. Add the cream and the remaining 3 teaspoons sugar to a large bowl. Whisk to soft peaks.

3. Add the reserved berries to the cream and very gently fold them in a few times so that lots of streaks of berries remain. Serve immediately.

Honey Whip

Sweet and delicate

MAKES ABOUT 2 CUPS

1 cup (240ml) chilled heavy cream

2 tablespoons runny honey

Add the cream and honey to a large bowl. Whisk to soft peaks and serve immediately.

Orange Blossom Whip

Sweet and floral

MAKES ABOUT 2 CUPS

1 cup (240ml) chilled heavy cream

1 tablespoon sugar

2 teaspoons orange blossom water

Add the cream, sugar, and orange blossom water to a large bowl. Whisk to soft peaks and serve immediately.

Vanilla Bean Whip

Smooth and sweet

MAKES ABOUT 2 CUPS

1 cup (240ml) chilled heavy cream

2 teaspoons sugar

2 teaspoons vanilla bean paste

Add the cream, sugar, and vanilla bean paste to a large bowl. Whisk to soft peaks and serve immediately.

Whipped Ricotta
with Honey

Creamy and sweet

MAKES ABOUT 2 CUPS

1 cup (220g) full-fat ricotta

3 tablespoons runny honey

Add the ricotta and honey to a large bowl. Whisk vigorously until light and fluffy. Serve immediately or store in the fridge, covered, for a few hours. Stir before serving.

Whipped Vanilla Mascarpone

Fluffy and buttery

MAKES ABOUT 2 CUPS

1 cup (225g) mascarpone

1 tablespoon sugar

1 teaspoon vanilla bean paste or vanilla extract

Add the mascarpone, sugar, and vanilla to a large bowl. Whisk until light and fluffy and serve immediately.

a sprinkle for every cake

Feel free to sprinkle your glazed and frosted cakes with abandon. Make sure to add the sprinkles while the glaze or frosting is still wet or they won't stick. Here are some ideas to get you started.

CANDY-COATED CHOCOLATES

CHOPPED OR SHAVED CHOCOLATE

CHOPPED PRETZELS

CHOPPED TOASTED NUTS

COCOA NIBS (THE CHOCOLATE-COVERED ONES ARE ESPECIALLY GOOD)

CRUSHED CORNFLAKES

CRUSHED POTATO CHIPS

FREEZE-DRIED FRUIT

FRESH FRUIT

SEEDS

SPRINKLES

TOASTED COCONUT

VALRHONA PEARLS

acknowledgments

Many thanks to my wonderful and supportive partner, Pete, who truly held down the fort during the months of this book's creation. Thank you for your patience and unwavering love and support during this process, and always.

Thank you to my parents for your love and support.

I feel so fortunate to have been able to make this book with the incredibly talented team at Clarkson Potter. Many thanks to Jenn Sit for encouraging me to take on this project and to Alyse Diamond and Raquel Pelzel for seeing it through to the finish.

Thank you to Mia Johnson for your beautiful and thoughtful design, and thank you to Stephanie Huntwork for your incredibly helpful insights. It was such a treat to work with you. To everyone else at Clarkson Potter who contributed to this fun project, thank you so much.

Many thanks to my agent Kari Stuart for helping me in every possible way, and for being such a kind and thoughtful sounding board for my many, many questions.

Thank you, Jim, for your expert guidance.

Ali Slagle, I absolutely could not have done this without you. Your keen insight throughout this whole process from testing to photo shoot was immeasurably helpful, and it is truly my honor to call you my friend and collaborator.

To Lauryn Bodden, the fastest baker in the east, I could not have made it through the shoot without you. Lucy Lamboy, thank you so much for stepping in and getting us started.

To Peter Bagi and Rype Studio. Your generosity is unmatched, thank you.

To the generous artists at Beau Rush Ceramics, Candice Boese, Meilen Ceramics, Noble Plateware, and Falcon Enamelware. Thank you so, so much for trusting me with your wares. They made the photographs for this book so special and beautiful.

Thank you to Erin Clarkson for letting me raid your sifter and cooling rack stash.

Thank you to all of the recipe testers who took time to generously and enthusiastically bake from this book. There were so many of you, and your feedback was so incredibly valuable and enlightening: Kelly, Yousef, Keira, Liv, Sophy, Janie, Danielle, Fahren, Marce and Lauren, Ali and Sheri, Jumee, Claire, Carole, Cathie, Saunders and Jennifer, Molly, Rosie, Amy and Leslie, Sarah, Julie, Andrea, and Alanna and Jack.

To my most prolific testers, Susan Arefi and Janet Farnan, extra kudos to you. You have baked more recipes from this book than just about anyone, and I appreciate your love and support so very much.

To all of my friends and neighbors who provided generous feedback as I worked through these recipes, thank you for your thoughts and encouragement.

And to the readers and supporters of Apt. 2B Baking Co., I owe you all so much. Thank you.

metric conversion chart

1 cup all-purpose flour	128g
1 cup whole wheat flour	130g
1 cup cocoa powder	90g
1 cup granulated sugar	200g
1 cup brown sugar	200g
1 cup confectioners' sugar	100g
1 cup liquid	240ml
1 cup yogurt	220g
1 cup sour cream	220g
1 cup ricotta cheese	220g
1 cup chopped nuts	100g
1 cup chopped chocolate or chips	170g
1 cup butter (2 sticks)	226g
1 stick butter	113g

index

Note: Page references in *italics* indicate photographs.